HOW TO ACT & EAT AT THE SAME TIME

The Business of Landing A Professional Acting Job

By Tom Logan

HOW TO ACT & EAT AT THE SAME TIME

The Business of Landing A Professional Acting Job

By Tom Logan

Communications Press, Inc.
Washington, D.C.

Grateful acknowledgment is made to the American Federation of Television and Radio Artists for permission to reprint the list of its locals and chapters; to Actors' Equity Association for permission to reprint the list of its offices, the list of theatres participating in its Membership Candidate Program, and the eligibility requirements for joining Equity; to the Screen Actors Guild for permission to reprint the list of its offices, the eligibility requirements for joining SAG, and the distribution of earnings figures for SAG members. Grateful acknowledgment also is made to the following actors for permission to reprint their photographs: Susan Blu, Deanna Lynn, Sam Nickens, Mary Saxon, and Kip Waldo; to the photographers: John Gibson, Sean Kenney, Buddy Rosenberg, and Tama Rothschild; and to Anderson Graphics for its design and graphics presentation of composites.

Communications Press, Inc.
1346 Connecticut Avenue, N.W.
Washington, D.C. 20036

ISBN: 0-89461-038-4
ISBN: 0-89461-039-2 (pbk)

Cover design by Linda McKnight

Printed in the United States of America

First Printing November 1982
Second Printing January 1983
Third Printing January 1984
Fourth Printing September 1985

This book is dedicated to the people in the
entertainment industry who have helped me over the years,
And to my parents, Margaret and George,
for their very special love.

CONTENTS

EXHIBITS

FOREWORD

For those of you who have heard that the world of entertainment is a "dream factory," learn now that it is a business, a business of knowledge, talent, hard work, some heartbreaks, and sometimes great rewards.

Tom Logan, in *How to Act and Eat at the Same Time,* presents a factual handbook for achieving the ultimate goal—success as a performer. This book should be read and used by professional as well as beginning actors as a guideline. I believe that it is an actor's responsibility to be aware of the business as a business; with this book you can organize yourself step-by-step to pursue your goals with discipline and professionalism.

Tom takes you right from the beginning. As in any field, getting your "roots" is very important. Tom's book covers these areas in excellent detail, whether your goals are Broadway, Hollywood, or other cities where professional actors work. The young neophite actor, out of anxiety and eagerness, leaves himself/herself open to a lot of misinformation and possible rip-offs. This book aids in rubbing off some of the "green"—pointing out many of the pitfalls to look out for and helping the actor to proceed, and realize the importance of proceeding, on solid ground.

As a casting director for both major motion pictures and television shows, I've interviewed thousands of actors. And, believe me, it's that professional attitude that impresses me most. If actors come in and hand a casting director a stack of pictures all disorganized and with no resumes, and they want to sit down and write their credits out on the picture, obviously that lack of discipline is going to carry over to acting discipline. Even if someone does not have a lot of credits, if he or she has an attitude of professionalism, a kind of coordination, I am more apt to be receptive to that person than I am to someone who is totally disorganized.

Sometimes that same kind of disorganization is found in agents. So you should be very careful in choosing one to represent you. And it's up to you to make sure the agent is properly acquainted with your talents and credits. Additionally, you have to be in tune with what's going on in the business—what kinds of shows are being cast, by whom, where, etc., and which of them are more likely to use your type—so that you at least can say, "I know such-and-such project is going on." The agent, because he or she handles other people and other projects, may not be aware of *everything* that's right for you.

With this book, you are going to learn how to organize *your* career. You are going to find detailed, nitty-gritty advice on photographs, resumes, unions, searching for agents, dealing with agents, casting, and much more. I have cast Tom in shows and I know personally of his professionalism as an actor. That same professionalism carries over into this book—a disciplined approach, attention to detail and accuracy, strong organization, and a good attitude. Tom's sense of humor (a valuable attribute for the professional actor) makes HOW TO ACT AND EAT AT THE SAME TIME *fun* to read. To paraphrase Charlton Heston, in his comment about this book, Tom writes not only with *wisdom,* but with *wit.*

In the past I've been asked if there is a Marvin Paige recipe for an actor. There is: know your craft. It's more than just your acting ability; it's that plus the *business* of landing a professional acting job, explained in the following pages. Add to that some of your own "magic" and some luck and you're on your way.

Marvin Paige

Marvin Paige is one of Hollywood's top casting directors. He has cast for such major studios as 20th Century Fox, Warner Bros., Paramount, and MGM. He has cast many motion pictures including "Star Trek—The Motion Picture," "The Man with Bogart's Face," "Breakfast at Tiffany's," "Take the Money and Run," and "Everything You Always Wanted to Know About Sex," as well as many television series including "Combat," "Branded," "Lassie," "Tarzan," "Planet of the Apes," and the currently top-rated ABC daytime series "General Hospital."

PREFACE

In starting into any profession, one needs to recognize that many approaches may be taken. This book represents MY opinions and recommendations, formulated over the course of my experience in the acting profession. My goal is to guide the amateur actor turning professional. Acting is a very difficult profession—not for the faint of heart—and I hope to help you avoid making costly, and sometimes disastrous, mistakes.

In this book, I've included some samples of photos, resumes, and letters. The photos are of real, working actors, as you will likely recognize when you view them. The resumes and letters were composed as models for this book; to all you Bill Rays and Joe Smiths out there, it's only a coincidence that I used your name. The fees and payments cited herein are, of course, subject to change. But they are applicable as we go to press in the fall of 1982, and likely will obtain with little or no change for at least another two or three years.

To all you aspiring actresses: Until the language includes a solution better than such usage as "s/he," "he/she," "actor/actress," and the like, I shall adhere to the traditional usage of the masculine gender when referring to both sexes. My publisher, a woman, agrees.

I contacted numerous people in the business to give me this technical idea and that technical opinion. There are definitely too many who helped me to mention all their names. But there are a few that must be mentioned, or I would be unable to sleep at night. I wish to personally thank Rob Tunnicliff and George Ives of the New York and Hollywood, Actors' Equity Association offices, respectively, and Mark Locher of the Screen Actors Guild. They have all spent numerous hours explaining to me the technical information used herein concerning their respective unions.

I also wish to thank Norman Ware for his terrific editorial assistance. And, most importantly, I wish to thank Executive Editor and Publisher of Communications Press, Mary Louise Hollowell. Thank you, Mary Louise, for your patience, editorial guidance, constant pressure for accuracy, moral support, and, of course, your strong belief in what I am trying to accomplish in this book.

INTRODUCTION

Please do me a favor: Don't read this book with false expectations. I'm not going to tell you who's sleeping with whom, or who's having whose baby. And I'm not going to tell you about how, in just ten easy steps, actors have attained stardom overnight. If you're interested in such stories, then read some of the popular magazines and newspapers that you can pick up each week at your local supermarket check-out counter. I just hope you don't put much faith in those publications. Keep in mind that they interview people who have been taken aboard spaceships, people with intellectual by-passes who have been reincarnated from some animal, and fly-by-night doctors who prescribe astrology for birth control. My book contains no such stories.

This isn't a "how to act" book either. If you don't already have the experience you need for this business, then put this book on "hold" and go get the experience. *Then* this book can be of great service to you.

No matter how much talent you have, you need to know some basic things about getting started as an actor or actress. (Herein "actor" and "actress" will be referred to as "actor.") Otherwise, you can get yourself into a lot of the trouble that actors get themselves into every day.

1

SHOW BUSINESS is two words—SHOW and BUSINESS. If you are reading this book, you probably have the SHOW part under control. Perhaps you've got your degree in acting from Shakespeare University. Or you've taken so many acting, singing, and dancing courses that you could now start your own school. Or maybe you're the star in your hometown but you just haven't quite made the step to professional acting. Or you've completed your acting studies and have been waiting tables for two years at a restaurant frequented by directors and producers, hoping to be "discovered." If you fit into any of these or similar categories, this book was written for you.

You must know the BUSINESS and know it well. ACTING IS A BUSINESS. It's very easy to get "ripped off" when pursuing a professional acting career. Actors are ripped off every day, every hour, every minute. How do I know this happens? Well, I have plenty of hungry, out-of-work actor-friends who make their living off actors like yourself who don't know how to go about starting an acting career.

This book will help you to stay ahead of the con artists. Believe me, they're out there. They aren't underworld figures or Mafia types. They have white houses with white picket fences, and station wagons with wood on the sides. They will give you all kinds of promises for success. They will try to take money from you. After reading my book, however, you will have no doubt in your mind as to whom you should give money, when, and for what reasons.

Do I fault my con-artist friends? No! The fault lies with the actors who are so starstruck that they fall for a lot of get-rich schemes in which only the cons get rich. These con artists know that there are no easy ways to make it as an actor. Forget all the promises that people will make, and plow ahead with good business sense. It may not be easy, but YOU CAN WORK AS AN ACTOR AND EAT AT THE SAME TIME.

First, you need to make sure your attitude is *serving* you rather than hurting you. Then you'll need to get photos of yourself and compose a resume and cover letter, to submit to agents. And you must learn how to *find* a good agent in your field, and how to *deal* with the agent. You will of course want to get a real understanding of how a role is cast in "big time" TV, film, and theatre. And you won't want to neglect consideration of acting in TV commercials.

All of these subjects are covered in some detail in this book. Among the Exhibits are samples of photographs, resumes, and letters. Also given are union eligibility requirements and lists of offices and organizations that could be important to your professional acting career.

You would eventually learn the information in this book for yourself by trial and error. That's how most actors find out about this business. I hope to save you time and money so that you can put your talents and training to work as soon as possible. In the process I hope to put some of my con-artist friends out of business. Then they'll have to make their living by acting, the legit way, like the rest of us.

When I first moved to Los Angeles and started looking for work as an actor, I looked for such a book as I have written here, to help guide me in my search for an acting career. I was unable to find one. Now that I'm working as an actor, I can more easily see the scams being played out on people who are just starting out in the acting profession. I had to learn through trial and error.

And so, I've been looking for a book like this to use in classes that I teach in Los Angeles at various studios. When students first enter my classes, I usually hear a few horror stories about all the money they have been contributing to my con friends—all to no avail. I've halted my search to find a simple practical guide to aid the beginning professional actor; I decided to write one myself. Don't just read this book. USE IT.

Chapter 1

SETTING THE FOUNDATION

An optimistic attitude. I guess you've heard all your life that you have to think positive to succeed at anything. Sit down, relax, and get ready to hear it again. My own warped version of this truism just might make the concept clearer to you:

When I was in college, still wet behind the ears, I always had to have proof of everything. I couldn't take anything for granted. During my senior year, I had to write a thesis for my final psychology project. I had already written all about the mating habits of the female frog and other interesting subjects, so I had to search very hard for something to top my previous efforts.

Finally I decided to test an old idea that I had never really believed in. To start the project, I rounded up three of my college buddies, all who were ready for any kind of mischief.

At ten o'clock in the morning I had one of my buddies pass by the secretary's office in the psychology department. This friend "just happened" to stroll into Beverly's office and strike up a conversation about the flu. Beverly and my friend conversed for a long time about how everyone was running out and receiving their flu shots, which were being given all over the country that year. Beverly mentioned that she had not received one of these shots and my friend advised her to do so as soon as possible. Beverly responded that she felt fine,

4

but would think about my friend's suggestion.

Around twelve noon that same day, I sent another devil to Beverly's office. This particular devil told Beverly that she looked pale and tired, and suggested that she start getting more sleep. Beverly responded that she had been a little tired all day, but that she felt okay.

Two o'clock rolled around and another buddy of mine strolled into the office and told Beverly that she looked as though she were coming down with that "terrible flu that everyone on campus has." My friend suggested a good doctor for Beverly to go see. Beverly responded that she hadn't been feeling well all day.

At four o'clock I (the worst devil of all) went into Beverly's office to pick up some papers for the next semester's registration. I mentioned to Beverly that she "should go home immediately" because she looked as though she could use the rest. I also mentioned that her face looked a little pale and that perhaps she should go to the campus hospital and have her temperature taken. I suggested that she do this at once, so that the rest of us wouldn't get infected.

Not only did Beverly leave at one minute after four that afternoon, but she didn't return for four days. Was Beverly really sick? Yes, but what was the cause?

Okay, I'm a devil. But there's a definite point to be made here: if you are told something, or tell yourself something, long enough, you tend to accept it as reality. Psychologists call this theory the "self-fulfilling prophesy." We'll call it the "Beverly Theory."

So by now you're wondering what the Beverly Theory has to do with acting. Everything! Your attitude could be the most important factor in your success or lack thereof in Hollywood, California, or Hollywood, Florida. If you believe that the actors who are working professionally are better than you, and you decide that you really don't have much of a chance against these veterans, then save yourself some time and give this book to a friend. Without a positive attitude, this book won't do you any good.

Start thinking right this minute that you'll be successful in this business. Don't doubt for one minute that you have what it takes to make your living as an actor. If you truly believe this, then you have one of the most important traits you'll need to become a professional actor . . . confidence!

When actors are uneasy on auditions, it shows in their readings; producers can tell. Your attitude should show the producers that you think you're the best person for that part. (But be careful: there's a difference between being assured and being cocky.)

Let's say you're a producer spending millions of dollars on a project and an actor comes in to read for you. This actor is obviously insecure. He's nervous. Perhaps he spent more time in the office bathroom than did the Tidy Bowl man. And you're resting thousands of dollars on him personally even for a small part. Would you take a chance with him or would you instead hire someone who came in to read with a certain air of confidence?

Ask yourself this: "Would I hire myself, were I the producer?" Consider the competition. Would you spend big bucks on a name actor, or an actor with a lot of credits, who you knew could do the job, or would you spend it on someone like yourself? If you yourself aren't confident that you can do the job and do it well, then don't expect studio executives and theatre producers to feel confident that you can.

You have enough going against you already by going into the acting profession. Everyone does, so don't add to it by showing the producer that you aren't the right person for the job. He can sense your confidence (or lack of it) after seeing you for only a few seconds. The moment you walk in the door, he is sizing you up.

You may be thinking to yourself now, "it's one thing to talk about 'confidence,' as if that were easy to come by; but what if I screw up? How can I *not* be uptight at that possibility?" Well, relax. You're an actor and a little embarrassment is an occupational hazard.

I remember interviewing for a Lipton Ice Tea commercial. During the interview I was standing on the diving board over a pool of water as the interviewers questioned my dancing and coordination abilities. I went on and on about my dancing routines in the musicals

"Mame" and "Applause." Suddenly, I tripped on the diving board and fell into the water. As I climbed back on the diving board and then walked away, chuckles could be heard from everyone, except me. But, believe me, within an hour after the incident, they had seen so many actors that my escapade was hardly remembered.

What is the worst thing that can happen on an audition? Making a fool of yourself? No! Being embarrassed? No! Breaking down in tears because your reading was so awful? No! The worst thing that can happen is that you don't get the part. And SO WHAT? You didn't have it when you walked in the door, so you really haven't lost anything, have you? It's not the end of your career. You'll have other auditions.

It's just a fact that no matter how good or bad you are on an audition, someone on that audition likely will do better than you and someone will do worse. The worst person on that interview probably won't get the role and the best person might not get the role either. Just accept the fact that you aren't going to be perfect on every audition. (I said *Accept it*—don't worry about it.) You'll give some good auditions and you'll give others that will leave a lot to be desired. And no matter how terrible you think a particular situation is, it can only become worse if you're not cautious of the Beverly Theory.

I remember my first TV show audition, which was for a Movie Of The Week for ABC. My reading had the producers laughing so hard that one of them fell out of his chair. This would have been fine, if the movie had been a comedy. But it was a serious drama and I was supposed to be crying in a funeral scene. The producer asked me my name and I was so unnerved, that I was stumped for an answer.

The producer even told me that my reading was "less than adequate." I left his office in tears, but the next day, I got the job! As pointed out earlier, it's important on an audition to have confidence and to show them that you can do the job. But in that particular case they were looking for a klutz and on that audition I was about as klutzy as they come. The point is, be as confident as you can, but if something goes wrong, it's not the end of the world.

Talent? Obviously the decision makers are sometimes just as confused as everyone else—for you can sit at home and watch your TV, go to a theatre to see a movie, or attend a stage play in New York, and see terrible and terrific performances by actors. Maybe they have a lot of talent and maybe they don't. But one thing they do have is a success-oriented personality.

And, if it'll make you feel any better, let me confirm something that you may already have heard: It really doesn't matter if you make a fool of yourself in, for example, some high-level TV executive's office. He probably won't have his job in six months anyway. The turnover in this business is unbelievable, so you'll always have another chance. Relax.

Attitude covers a lot of other areas as well. For example, too many actors sit around talking about how unfair the acting profession is. They're right! The acting profession isn't a fair business, never has been and never will be (what is, really?). Beverly will tell you that sitting around talking about how unfair it is will only make it more "unfair" where you are concerned. Bitterness and self-pity won't help you get work. Just accept the realities and get on with BUSINESS.

Attitude is also involved in the way you treat the people around you. Be strong, but be kind to other people. I haven't yet figured out why so many actors in press interviews admit how awful they are to their fellow human beings. Some actors talk about how they order everyone around on the set, and they comment on what big stars they are. I see no advantage in treating people like machines, and it's a strange coincidence that many of these same actors have a hard time finding work when, for example, their TV show is cancelled—which it ultimately will be! There's a long list of has-beens to verify this. An old saying in Hollywood that all of us need to keep in mind is BE NICE TO THE PEOPLE ON YOUR WAY UP BECAUSE YOU'RE GOING TO SEE THESE SAME PEOPLE ON YOUR WAY DOWN.

Logistics

The essentials for a healthy attitude are determination, hard work, a strong will, loads of confidence, respect for others, some luck, and a complete understanding of the Beverly Theory. But even actors can't live on an inspired attitude alone. There are a few other essentials for laying a foundation, which may seem obvious but which deserve at least a brief mention.

First of all, you'll need lodging. A street address is preferable, but if you're living in Central Park, at least get a post office box. If you're moving to Los Angeles or New York from a smaller city, you might be in for a real shock when looking for a place to live. If you're broke—normal status for many actors—looking for an apartment in those cities will probably rank on your "fun list" right up there with doing the laundry.

Since you are going to have to pay for that lodging and other necessities, you'll need an income. If you're not endowed with a comfortable inheritance, this means a job. Unfortunately, auditions are usually held in the daytime hours. So you either have to have a job that permits you to leave upon request during the day, or have a night job. Actors have all kinds of jobs, such as waiters, waitresses, insurance salesmen, mechanics, parole officers, etc.

You'll need a telephone. If there are no hook-ups on the tree under which you sleep, you'll at least need a friend with a phone, who will faithfully monitor your incoming calls.

Along with your telephone, you'll need an answering service. You can't do without one! You can't afford to miss a single call. There are all kinds of answering services. The least expensive type is one in which your callers call a central number that you frequently check. One of the most expensive types is one in which your home phone is connected to the answering service, where operators answer your own phone connection for you when you're out.

An answering machine is fine if you don't mind "hang-ups" from personal friends. Sometimes answering machines are more reliable than some of the answering services. If someone in the acting profession wants to reach you, he'll talk to your answering machine.

You basically need to have the appearance of a secure person. You don't want to appear as though you're a total failure as a human being. So find a place to live, have an income, and secure a telephone and an answering service of some type. Now that you are set as a resident of the community, we'll move on to the next step, PHOTOGRAPHS.

Chapter 2

GETTING PHOTOS OF YOURSELF

Every actor must have photographs of himself. Photographs (together with resumes) are passports for getting into agents' offices.

Be sure to have your pictures taken in the city in which you plan to work as an actor. If you're going to launch your career in New York, then pictures taken in Omaha won't do. The Omaha photographer doesn't know what is currently selling in New York. And, likewise, the New York photographer isn't as aware of what is selling in Hollywood as is the Hollywood photographer.

Splurge—go to a professional photographer who shoots actors for a living. But, be reasonable about price. If you can't decide whether to pay the photographer's fee or fly your family to Paris, you're probably being over-charged. It is best to check around to see what the price "norm" is in that particular city. Also, if the photographer shoots bar mitzvahs and weddings, I'd be careful. You don't want a jack-of-all-trades. You may have a harder time finding such a specialist in the smaller cities outside of New York and Los Angeles, but be persistant.

Don't go to just *any* photographer who claims to shoot actors for a living. DO YOUR RESEARCH. There are reliable sources of information on photographers, which are available in any city. The best source of information is from actors themselves. Word of mouth is always the best referral. Don't be afraid to ask around.

You can also get names of good photographers directly from agents' offices. Call a few agents' offices and ask the secretary what photographers they use for their clients. Be sure not to bother the agent himself; the secretary should have all the information you need.

If you're in New York you can find photographers' ads in "Backstage" and "Show Business," and if you're in Los Angeles you can look through "Drama-Logue," all of which are published weekly and can be purchased from most major newsstands in those cities. However, personal recommendations are always best. (We will be referring to these publications throughout the book, and keep in mind that even though the above publications may be distributed in other cities, their primary concern is with their particular geographical area.)

Before you decide on a particular photographer, be sure to request to see some of his work. Base your decision on what he can do, and not on what he tells you. If he's a good photographer, he'll be more than happy to show you other pictures he's taken of *actors*.

The important thing is to get fantastic pictures of yourself. Pictures taken in high school for the yearbook, or pictures that look like left-over mug shots from "60 Minutes," simply won't do. There's no substitute for the best pictures you can possibly get of yourself. You've come this far in your career. Spend a few extra bucks and go much further!

Basically, you can go two ways with your pictures; you can either get a "head shot" or a "composite," depending on which medium you're after. A head shot is essential, whatever the field. A composite is necessary for commercials, though some children's agents will use a composite, along with a head shot, for TV and film, as well as for commercial uses. In some of the smaller cities, many agents use composites for TV, film, and commercial uses for all their clients, though this being the case, most of them will still want you to have a head shot.

A head shot is just that—a shot of your face. A typical head shot is usually taken from the middle of the bustline or the shoulders up. (See examples in this chapter.) The photo should be an eight-by-ten glossy. If you go into an agent's office with five-by-seven photos, you're only displaying your own naiveté about the professional world of acting. And, polaroids and snapshots are a complete no-no.

Since the head shot will be presented to agents and producers with a resume attached to the back, having your name printed on the photo is optional. But it's highly recommended; if your picture and resume become separated in some agent's office, he'll be able to match them up again. The name should be printed at the bottom of the picture and in such a way as to make it very visible. Many actors have their name printed on a whited-out space, as opposed to having it printed directly on the picture image, giving it more recognition. If the photo image is dark at the bottom, however, then having your name printed in white lettering will have the same effect. (The opposite is also true.) Just be sure to have contrast between the lettering for your name and its background. Some actors, once they have an agent, like to have their agent's name printed on the bottom of the head shot, on the opposite side of their name.

A "composite" is a group of photos on one sheet. (See examples in this chapter.) Usually a composite consists of one photo on the front and three to five on the back. The front shot is usually a head shot; the back ones are usually full-length shots. Occasionally, actors put an interesting full-length shot on the front and include a smaller head shot on the back, along with the full-length shots. The total composite, which will be printed on graphic paper, will be eight-and-a-half by eleven inches in size.

Some children's agents occasionally like to combine the head shot and composite. In other words, the agent might have the actor put a head shot on an eight-and-a-half by eleven inches sheet of graphic paper, with an insert or two of smaller photos, usually in the lower half of the page. This combination composite/head shot should also include the actor's name at the bottom of the page.

The problem with making up a composite (or combination composite/head shot) at this point is that the agent you end up with might not like one of the photos. He might tell you to put together a new composite, and, in the process, you'll spend a lot more money. So, until you have an agent, concentrate on getting a good head shot.

Either way you go—head shot or composite—there are certain basic things to remember.

● The photos should be black-and-white only. Color is expensive, and I don't know any working actors who use it. High-fashion models might use color photos for modeling, but not for acting.

● All photos should be up-to-date. You probably no longer resemble the person in your high school pictures; you've lost all your freckles and your acne. You want to appear as though you've advanced beyond high school acting. An old picture taken at Disneyland with Donald Duck is cute, but not very professional.

● Your photos should be very "alive"; they should have a very "up" feeling. Smiles are always a plus. And a lot of action is a must in the commercial composite.

● It's a good idea to make an appointment with your photographer before the shooting, to discuss make-up, clothing, backgrounds, and other particulars. Decide these things beforehand so that the shooting can go smoothly. You waste the photographer's time and your money if you spend most of the afternoon discussing the particulars that should have been worked out in advance. You will have lost more "shooting time" with the photographer.

● The photos shouldn't be taken with gobs of make-up on your face. Make-up that is applied with a putty knife and removed with a chisel will only demonstrate what an amateur you are. Don't get just *any* make-up artist; find someone who knows what type of make-up you need for the particular field you're interested in. You can get information on make-up artists from photographers who are used to shooting actors.

The important thing to keep in mind is that make-up for your photos is different from street make-up. Make-up for all your acting photos should be very subtle. Wearing too much make-up in your photos makes you look phony.

EXHIBIT 1: Example of head shot

SUSAN BLU

Background is softly mottled, thus avoiding the "flat" look, and contrasting shade highlights her face and hair. Nice, natural smile.

Photo by Tama Rothschild

EXHIBIT 2: Example of combination head shot/composite

Note effective use of light around face in headshot, and lively activity in inset.

Photos by Sean Kenney

EXHIBIT 3: Example of Composite, Side One

Sam Nickens

Note his lively facial expression here and on other side, and variety of roles demonstrated.

Photo by John Gibson

EXHIBIT 3 (cont'd): Example of Composite, Side Two

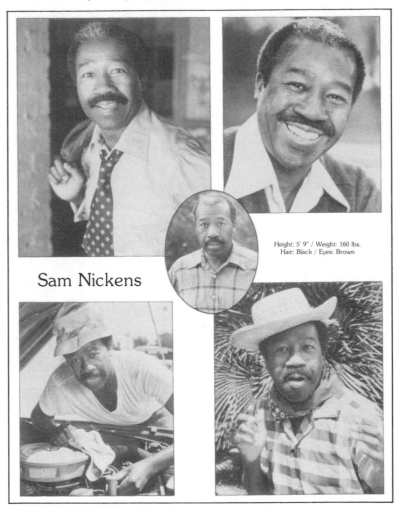

Sam Nickens

Height: 5' 9" / Weight: 160 lbs.
Hair: Black / Eyes: Brown

Photos by John Gibson

EXHIBIT 4: Example of Composite, Side One

Mary Saxon

Personable headshot, and, in photos on other side, camera catches actress in action in a number of realistic environments.

Photo by Buddy Rosenberg

EXHIBIT 4 (cont'd): Example of Composite, Side Two

Mary Saxon
SAG/AFTRA
Height: 5' 8" / Weight: 120 lbs.
Hair: Brown / Eyes: Brown

Photos by Buddy Rosenberg

EXHIBIT 5: Example of Composite, Side One

Kip Waldo

The "type" in this composite comes across immediately—and favorably.
Who wouldn't love the guy?

Photo by Buddy Rosenberg

EXHIBIT 5 (cont'd): Example of Composite, Side Two

Kip Waldo

Height: 5' 11"   Hair: Brown
Weight: 230 lbs.   Eyes: Brown

Photos by Buddy Rosenberg

Make-up for commercial photos should even be more subtle than that used for TV and film photos. You don't want to look like "an actor" in your photos. You want to look like the "everyday-person-next-door." "Everyday" looking people work much more frequently in commercials than do the "model" types, because of more public identity. If you're a gorgeous-model type, then your commercial photos should represent you as such, but keep the above in mind.

Make-up for the stage is thicker than that used for TV and films because, obviously, the audience is at a further distance. More lines are used under the eyes, around the nose, etc., because otherwise, the face becomes "lost" in the distance. However, your photos for stage work should be somewhat like the ones used for TV and films. The less make-up, the better. The point is, find a make-up person who knows the differences.

● Clothes, too, should be chosen carefully. Of course they should be clean. And they nccdn't be fancy; they should convey a down-to-earth, "everyday life" feeling. But don't get carried away; you don't want clothes that are so down-to-earth that they make you look as though you get your fashion tips from "Hee Haw."

Your clothes shouldn't draw attention away from your face. You can wear patterns on your shirts, but make sure they aren't distracting. Avoid plain all-white shirts; they tend to reflect light and thus cause glare in the photo. Wear a shirt which makes your face stand out; a shirt color which *contrasts* well with your skin color will most effectively do this.

● While paying so much attention to your face and clothes, don't forget about the background. Be careful that there are no distracting objects in the photo. For example, standing in front of a window sill with a potted plant in the window might make it appear as though the pot or plant is growing out of your head.

Phony indoor backdrops are a definite no-no; the photos should be taken outdoors, to avoid the "flat" look. Also, natural backgrounds give the picture a happier feeling, and a more "up" photo is more appealing.

● Many actors have different photos taken for different job

interviews. They may have a shot of themselves baling hay, for instance. Such a photo could be used to portray a "farmer" image. They may have a shot of themselves in a suit and tie. A suit and tie are generally too dressy for your photo, but could be used to portray a "businessman" image for an appropriate interview. You *eventually may* want different types of photos for different types of roles.

● Do your photos look posed? Or do they convey the feeling that someone just happened to walk by and take your picture? Producers can look at your photo and tell how natural you'll appear on camera. Agents know that if you can't pose naturally for a photo, you'll have a hard time looking natural in front of the TV-film camera or stage audience.

● The photos shouldn't look better than you really look. These shots aren't for the family album. If you need family pictures for Aunt Fanny and Uncle Bob, fine. But keep them in the family album and don't use them as professional acting photos. Likewise, your photographs shouldn't look worse than you really look. You're only cutting your own throat if your pictures don't accurately represent YOU.

These pictures will eventually be sent to agents and casting directors; if they like the physical "type" they see, they may call you in for an interview. Let's say you send your picture to an agent; in the picture you have blond hair, a perfect nose, and an angelic face. The agent loves the "type" he sees in your photo, so he calls you in for an interview. But when you walk in the door, you have dark hair, a ski-nose, and a face that would be less conspicuous in a zoo. The agent was looking for a specific type, and you've misrepresented yourself. You've wasted his time, and more importantly, your time.

In the same instance, what if another agent were looking for someone with dark hair, a ski-nose, and a face that looks like an aerial view of Mt. St. Helens? He certainly wouldn't call you, because in your photo you look beautiful and that's not what he wanted. You've cut your own throat because your photo didn't accurately represent you. "The camera takes a picture of what it sees." Bull! Make *sure* it sees you as you *are,* not as you'd like to be.

When You're Ready to Put Together a Composite

• For a commercial composite you'll want to use action photos. Swing a tennis racket; kick a soccer ball. Commercial situations can be effective, too. Perhaps a picture of you buying groceries at the supermarket is more your style.

• Be careful, however, NOT TO SHOW PRODUCT NAMES in your photos. If you go on an interview for a Coke commerical, and in your picture you're drinking 7-Up, there is an obvious conflict of interest. This probably won't prevent you from getting the Coke commercial, but it's safer not to photograph any product names.

• It's very important to have your name printed on your composite. (As you remember, this was optional on your head shot.) Once you have a commercial agent, this composite will be sent by your agent to casting directors, usually without a resume attached. Without your name on the composite, there would be no way to identify you. Your name should be printed on the top or bottom of the front picture and, as with the head shot, in most cases it's best to have the name printed on a whited-out area. Some actors also like to have their name printed on the back side in smaller letters.

• Many agents will want you to print your height, weight, and acting union affiliations. (Details on the unions will be provided later in this book.) If you're under eighteen years of age, they may want your birthdate and/or social security number on the composite. All this information should be printed on the back side of your composite.

• You'll need to go to a graphics store to have your composite put together. Be sure that the folks there do work for actors, and request to see some of their work; DO YOUR RESEARCH.

• Remember, if you're not working in New York or Los Angeles, many agents will want you to have a composite for TV, film, and stage, as well as for commercial interviews. Check with professionals in the town in which you plan to work to find out exactly what you'll need.

Once you have taken the pictures and have decided which one you want to use for your head shot, have it duplicated. (Save the contact sheets, or "proof sheets" as they are called in the acting business; they can be helpful to you when you're being interviewed by an agent, which we'll discuss in Chapter 5.) Go to a special photography store that mass-duplicates pictures; in the larger cities there are certain photo labs which cater to actors. You can find out about such services from other actors, your photographer, and agents. The yellow pages of the telephone directory generally isn't a good place to find such services. As when looking for a good photographer, personal referrals are preferred.

You'll need at least a hundred of these head shots if you're looking for an agent in New York or Hollywood. In the smaller cities, of course, you'll need fewer, for the time being.

So now you have a marvelous photograph of yourself. Do you take several copies of it and start knocking on producers' doors? No. You simply *must* have an agent. But before you go looking for an agent, first you need a RESUME to go along with your head shot. Your resume is the subject of the next chapter.

Chapter 3

COMPOSING A GOOD RESUME

So you worked at McDonald's for four years in a row, and you are thinking how wonderful this experience will look on your resume. Or perhaps you were a foreman at the Ford plant in your hometown, and executives there told you to use them as references. NO-NO. These references will be of no help whatsoever on your acting resume. Producers won't be hiring you for anything except acting, and they don't care what your previous employers think of you. Producers care about what *they* think of you and what *you* think of you.

You say that in your local play productions you have worked the light board and the sound board, and have taken tickets at the theatre door. You were probably told how important it was to learn all aspects of the theatre. I perfectly agree. It's important for an actor to know what is going on around him. However, if you want to be an actor, your resume should contain information about *acting only*. You probably won't ever see the lighting board, you probably won't understand the sound board, and no producer is going to hire you to take tickets at the door. In fact, in TV and film work, if you lift a prop, touch a light, or do anything with any equipment without being a member of a technical union, you could have a grievance filed against you by that union. According to the unions, you are taking somebody else's job away from him. Producers care about what you can do in *front* of the camera and stage, not behind them.

So you say, "I don't *have* any acting credits." Then get some! I am taking it for granted that you have already been through your initial training period. If you don't have any credits, then your professional resume will be a blank sheet of paper. (Some solutions to this problem are outlined later in this chapter.)

DO NOT LIE ABOUT ANY CREDITS! One way or another you'll get caught. An actor friend of mine named Sam told a TV producer that he had been on an episode of "Bionic Woman." The producer decided that he wanted to view the episode to see how my friend looked on film, and to see how his acting came across on the screen. The producer then phoned Universal Studios, where the "Bionic Woman" show was originally shot, and arranged a screening. The producer sat there for an hour watching the show, and Sam never appeared. This was a waste of the producer's time, and my friend's reputation with that producer is probably a notch below that of a child molester.

Your resume should be ONE PAGE ONLY. You don't want a lot of fat in it; and you don't want a resume that looks as though it has been "padded." Note from the samples included here that you do not have to follow one exact form or wording for your resume. But *do* be consistent in form and clear in presentation.

● At the top of the page, type your name, home address, home phone number, and answering service number, if different from your home number. Your resume initially will be sent to agents, and the agents need to know how to get in touch with you. Once you have an agent, NEVER LIST YOUR OWN ADDRESS OR PHONE NUMBER ON YOUR RESUME AGAIN; instead list your agent's name (or agency), address, and phone number. Your agent will be sending your pictures and resumes all over the city, and you'll have no idea who will see them. You won't want some big-city pervert to call you on the phone at home. Let him call your agent, and let your agent deal with him—that's part of the agent's job.

● Below your name you'll list some important items. Some

actors, if they're over eighteen, like to list their "Age Range." This is the range of ages that one can possibly play. It doesn't matter how old you actually are (so long as you are not a minor)—the crucial matter is how old or young you appear to be. The younger you are, the smaller your age range will be. Examples of age ranges could be 7-10, 15-20, 30-40, 60-75, etc. Of course these are only examples and your age range could fall anywhere in between these numbers, *within reason.* Few people, if any, can play 15-30, for example.

However, my personal opinion is that an actor should NEVER list his age range on his resume. Many agents and casting directors feel, and I certainly agree with them, that listing your age range puts you into a category and limits your selling ability.

If you're under eighteen years of age, once you have an agent, he might want you to list your birthdate on your resume. It all depends on the agent and his personal beliefs about what ages he thinks you can play. Until you have an agent, list your birthdate. However, anyone *over* eighteen years of age should NEVER list his age or birthdate.

Whatever you do, please don't represent yourself as being over eighteen if you're not. The studios will find out anyway when you start working for them, because of the Child Labor Laws in the state in which you're working. You will eventually mess up an entire shooting schedule on a TV show, film, commercial, or play if you're dishonest about being a minor.

That problem came up when I was working on a Movie Of The Week for TV with an actor named John. He had represented himself as being over eighteen years of age, but in reality he was only seventeen. The entire shooting schedule had to be altered because of the strict laws regarding the use of a minor. He cost the production company mucho bucks and time. Even though he's now over eighteen, it's a sure bet that he'll never work for that company again. The sad thing is that he might have been hired anyway, even if they had known he was under eighteen. The shooting schedule could have been worked differently at the outset to accomodate a minor.

Next list your "Height" and "Weight." If you're eight feet tall and so big you can only play seek, then represent yourself as such; so much the better. All types are needed for stage, TV, film, and commercials, and anything that makes you stand out from the crowd could be a plus.

There's an interesting point to be made here. TV will add about ten pounds to your appearance. Movies in the theatre will add a little less, but they too will put weight on you. "How is that?" you ask. Have you ever seen the picture tube inside your TV? It bends around the edges. This bending will stretch you out, and, by doing so, will add weight to you. Movies in the theatre will add weight, too, because the movie theatre screen is wider than it is tall. This does not mean, however, that you should add that extra weight to your statistic on the resume. Just keep in mind that TV, film, and commercial producers are very aware of the appearance of extra poundage.

● Next you'll list "Eyes" and "Hair." This category is less important for stage resumes than for screen resumes, but I think it's generally a good idea to list this information on any beginning acting resume.

● If you're a member of the Screen Actors Guild (SAG), the American Federation of Television and Radio Artists (AFTRA), or Actor's Equity Association (known as "Equity" or AEA), you'll want to mention which ones. (These unions, and related ones, will be discussed in detail in Chapter 4.) If you have some important TV, film, and stage credits with good billing, however, then obviously you're a member of the acting unions and can leave this category off your resume.

● If your resume is for TV, film, and commercials, you'll next want to list any "Television" and "Film" credits that you might have. You'll also want to include the production company that shot the show and any impressive billing you might have had—Star, Guest Star, Co-Star, Feature, etc. Generally it's not important to list the character you played on a TV show or feature film, unless, for some reason, people would identify with the character name; for instance, you were a regular on a popular TV series, or you were a very memorable character in a top grossing film.

Under "films" you can also list any university film productions you've been in. These credits obviously don't carry nearly as much weight as those of feature films for the theatres, but at least they will show the producers that you have worked in front of the camera.

Any film or tape that you have available of yourself—be it TV, feature film, university film, etc.—should be mentioned as "Tape Available," or "Film Available," in some prominent spot on your resume. Even though your scenes should be transferred to videotape if they're on film, the actor's industry jargon tends to refer to this as having "film on yourself." However, mention it as "Tape Available" if the scene(s) are put on videotape. (University productions, "film on yourself," and preparing your videotape for agents are covered in more detail in Chapter 4.)

● Next you might want to list any "Commercials" you've been in. This is optional; it depends on how many credits you have. Remember, your resume shouldn't be longer than one page, and the page shouldn't look crowded. If you have only three lines of TV and film credits, and you've acted in twenty commercials, go ahead and list your commercials. On the other hand, if you have a lot of TV and film credits, you might want to omit listing commercials altogether. Many actors who have a lot of professional credits simply state: "Commercials: List Available Upon Request."

● Following "Commercials" is the "Stage Roles" category. (Note: if your resume is to be used for stage, then list the category of "Stage Roles" before you list "Television" and "Film" roles.) Under the "Stage Roles" category, list the play, production company (theatre), and the role you played, if the resume is to be used for stage. If the resume is to be used for the screen and you have a few good TV and film credits, then it's optional whether or not to list the character you played; base your decision on the available space on your resume. Keep in mind that on a screen resume, stage credits don't carry as much weight as TV and film credits. But the stage is good training ground for TV and film, so professional stage credits can be useful.

EXHIBIT 6: Sample of Basic Stage Resume

BILL RAY

Joe Smith Agency
2000 Some Street
Hollywood, CA 90000

Height: 5'5"   Eyes: Hazel
Weight: 120   Hair: Blonde
                                                   SAG, AFTRA, EQUITY

Stage Roles:

FIDDLER ON THE ROOF   Fyedka   Performing Arts Center, Miami
THE MISER   Harpegon   Guthrie Theatre, Chicago
THE GUEST   Bill   The Dinner Theatre, NYC
CHILD'S PLAY   John   The Dinner Theatre, NYC
MAME   Mr. Babcock   The Arts Theatre, NYC

Television:

CHIPS   (Co-Star)   MGM
JAMES AT 16 (Star)   20th Century Fox

Film:

MR. SMITH   (Co-Star)   Bill Smith Productions
THE SPIDER   (Feature)   Jim Robards Productions

Theatrical Training:

Performing Arts Center   New York
Performance Workshop   Los Angeles
Children's Theatre Class   New York

Special Abilities:

Water-skiing
Fencing
Horseback riding
Motorcycle riding

EXHIBIT 7: Sample of Basic TV & Film Resume

BILL RAY

Joe Smith Agency
2000 Some Street
Hollywood, CA 90000

Height: 5'5"   Eyes: Hazel
Weight: 120   Hair: Blonde
                                                        SAG, AFTRA, EQUITY

Television:

    CHIPS   (Co-Star)   MGM
    HART TO HART   (Guest-Star)   Universal

Film:

    THE CLAM THAT ATE GRAMPS (Feature)   Bill Smith Productions

Commercials:

    JACK-IN-THE-BOX
    McDONALD'S
    PEPSI
    CREST TOOTHPASTE
    FORD
    RIGHT GUARD

Stage Roles:

    FIDDLER ON THE ROOF   Fyedka   Performing Arts Center, Miami
    THE MISER   Harpegon   Guthrie Theatre, Chicago
    THE GUEST   Bill   The Dinner Theatre, NYC
    CHILD'S PLAY   John   The Dinner Theatre, NYC

Theatrical Training:

    Performing Arts Center, NYC
    Performance Workshop, LA
    Children's Theatre Class, NYC

Special Abilities:

    Tennis
    Guitar
    Piano
    Drums
    Motorcycle riding

EXHIBIT 8: Sample of Advanced TV & Film Resume

BILL RAY
Joe Smith Agency
2000 Some Street
Hollywood, CA 90000

Height: 5'5"   Eyes: Hazel
Weight: 120   Hair: Blonde

TELEVISION:
    HART TO HART   (GUEST STAR)   Universal
    CHIPS   (CO-STAR)   MGM
    DUKES OF HAZZARD   (CO-STAR)   Warner Bros.
    BIONIC WOMAN   (GUEST STAR)   Universal
    RHODA   (CO-STAR)   MTM
    BOB NEWHART   (Feature)   MTM
    DIFFERENT STROKES   (Feature)   Tandem
    THE HARDY BOYS   (CO-STAR)   Universal
    YOUNG AND RESTLESS   Corday Productions
    DAYS OF OUR LIVES   Corday Productions
    WHAT'S HAPPENING   (Feature)   Tandem
    ALL IN THE FAMILY   (CO-STAR)   Tandem
    STARSKY AND HUTCH   (Feature)   20th Century Fox

FILM:
    ARTHUR   (Feature)   Orion
    BENJI   (CO-STAR)   Mulberry Square Productions
    POM POM GIRLS   (Feature)   Crown International
    1941   (Feature)   Universal

COMMERCIALS AND INDUSTRIAL FILMS:
    List available upon request

STAGE ROLES INCLUDE:
    THE GLASS MENAGERIE   TOM   Detroit Playhouse
    MY DAUGHTER'S RATED X   RALPH   Dallas Theatre
    MIDSUMMER NIGHT'S DREAM   PUCK   NATIONAL TOUR
    JESUS CHRIST SUPERSTAR   JESUS   NATIONAL TOUR

THEATRICAL TRAINING:
    JACK WRIGHT'S WORKSHOP   Dallas (2 years)
    PERFORMING ARTS SCHOOL   Miami (1 year)
    B.A. degree -- LSU   Baton Rouge (4 years)
    Vocal Training (John Busik)   Dallas (3 years)
    BURT SMITH'S DANCE ACADEMY   Los Angeles (2 years)

SPECIAL ABILITIES:
    Singing
    Dancing
    Horseback riding
    Water-skiing

Usually it's not a good idea to list "understudy" roles, unless you actually went on stage playing the role you understudied, and then you'd just list it as a regular role instead of an understudy role. However, the decision whether or not to list understudy roles as such, should be based on its status and on the number of other credits you might have. If you were understudying some name actor in a name show, this would carry a lot of weight. Also, if you don't have any credits other than understudy ones, then list them in the "Stage Roles" category. Next to the name of the show, list the name of the character you played and write "(understudy)" next to it. If you have a lot of understudy roles, and very few regular roles, then you might want to list the understudy ones in a separate category heading named "Understudy Roles," between the category of "Stage Roles" and the next category.

No matter what medium the resume is being used for, school and community plays carry very little weight on your professional acting resume. You must realize that when you auditioned for those plays you were auditioning against other people from local areas. Now you're in a whole new ball game—you're not just up against locals, you're up against stars with household names. *But,* if you don't have any professional acting credits, then it's okay to list any college dramatic productions or community theatre plays you performed in.

• The next category you'll want to list is "Theatrical Training" (which also includes vocal training and/or dancing instruction). Don't bother to list any high school drama courses; no one in the professional acting arena cares. College training is okay to list, but professional acting workshops are preferable. I suggest getting into a professional acting workshop in the city where you plan to work, if you're just starting out. You may wish to look through issues of "Backstage" and "Show Business" in New York, and "Drama-Logue" in Los Angeles, to find out about workshops. But you really should check with other actors, theatre groups, agents, photographers, etc., to learn which workshops are worth attending.

• Lastly, list any "Special Abilities" you have. This category is more important for a screen resume than it is for a stage resume;

you'll be performing more activities on the screen than on stage. (Exception: Singing and dancing abilities are extremely important on a stage resume.) You should list such things as snow skiing, high diving, ice skating, trumpet playing, horseback riding, guitar playing, singing, dancing, and so on. Being able to sing and dance are real pluses; the more talents a person can perform, the more roles he'll be able to audition for. Under this category be sure to list anything you do that is unique. You'd be surprised how important these special abilities can be. An actor friend of mine, who'd had no previous acting experience, landed a small part in a Movie Of The Week because when his agent sent his picture and resume to the casting director of the show, the casting director noticed that he could surf.

• DO NOT LIST ANY SCREEN "EXTRA" CREDITS ON A PROFESSIONAL RESUME in New York or Los Angeles, even if you don't have any other professional acting credits. Unless producers are hiring you to be an extra, and unless this is the career you wish to pursue, producers hiring you in those cities want to know what roles you've acted in where you "talked."

In fact, I recommend that you do *not* do any screen extra work in Los Angeles if you want to be a professional actor. The idea that one starts out as an extra and then moves his way up is generally hogwash. If you want to be a screen extra and make a career out of it, and frankly many extras make more money over the course of the year than do speaking players because the former usually work much more, then extra work is fine. But it isn't a good idea for the actor who wants to be known as an actor to become associated with extra work.

However, since New York is a theatre town, it isn't detrimental to your career to do screen extra work there if you're just starting out. Many actors who are looking for theatre acting jobs supplement their income with extra work. However, as stated above, extra work in New York, as well as Los Angeles, shouldn't be listed on your resume.

As for the cities other than the main production centers of Los Angeles and New York, many times out-of-town production companies will cast extra and small roles from local talent. Having screen extra credits on your resume will at least show them that you've been on a set, and this is generally important to them. But it's always best to check with other actors and some agents in that town to see what the norm is concerning the listing of extra credits.

Extra work for the *stage* is almost non-existent, and when there *is* a need for nonspeaking roles, they are usually filled by understudies for larger roles, who therefore are not considered extras. Understudy work is very beneficial and highly recommended. Many times the star has not been able to fulfill his duties on a particular night, and the understudy has "gone on" and gotten his big break. Whether to list understudy roles on your resume is an individual decision, as we discussed earlier.

* * * * * * *

When you finish writing your resume, you might find that it has much less information on it than you originally imagined; no one started out with a lot of professional acting credits. Every professional working actor had a first professional acting job, and you'll be no different. As time goes by, you'll accumulate more credits and your resume will look more and more impressive— because you're going to practice the "Avis Rent-A-Car Theory": TRY HARDER.

Type your resume very neatly, and then have it duplicated. You'll need as many copies of your resume as you have head shots. If you're starting out in New York or Los Angeles, you'll need at least a hundred to begin with. I am suggesting that you'll probably be sending a picture and resume to many, many agents in the town you plan to work, because you'll probably get fewer responses than you imagine. And, besides that, even after you obtain an agent, you'll need to give him many pictures and resumes to send to the studios. Most agents have a sticker which contains their name, office address, and phone number which they can place over your address and phone number at the top of your old resume. This will give you time to have more resumes printed containing your agent's name, address, and phone number.

You can have resumes printed very cheaply; check the yellow pages in your phone book and call some of the printers for their rates. Or look around for those "quickie" printing shops that usually advertise both photocopying and printing. Photocopying is slightly cheaper in most cases, but the difference is probably so little that the printing route is likely the better one to take. If you do choose to photocopy your resume, be sure to use a good machine; you don't want poor reproductions.

Staple your resume to the back of your head shot so that when you turn the picture over you can read your resume (in other words, back-to-back). Use only two staples, in the top two corners. Paper clipping resumes is a no-no. Agents and casting directors will be looking over your pictures and resumes very quickly and chances are your picture might be separated from your resume if they aren't stapled together.

Now that you have a fantastic photograph of yourself and a professional resume, we'll move on to the person with the most important influence on your career outside of yourself—YOUR AGENT.

Chapter 4

SEARCHING FOR AN AGENT

Before you begin your search for an agent, you may as well know that YOUR AGENT CAN'T PROMISE YOU WORK. There are no guarantees. Legit agents won't even give you the guarantee that they'll send you on *one* interview or audition. They themselves have no way of knowing how many, if any, they can get you in on. Your agent's job is not to get you work—that's your job! Your agent's job is to get your pictures and resumes into the hands of as many producers and casting directors as possible. Your agent will "follow up" your picture and resume with phone calls trying to get you in on the audition or interview. He will then negotiate your contracts with employers and take care of any business problems you have while working on the particular acting job. (You may be dealing with an individual agent, or with one working for a larger agency. In the latter case, you may actually have more than one agent working on your behalf. In either case, in industry jargon, you'd refer to your *agent,* in the singular.)

You can't exist without an agent in Hollywood. In New York it is a little easier to exist without one, but my suggestion is to start looking for an agent no matter what large city you're operating from. You have no way of knowing everything that is being cast in that city. Even if you had a direct source of such information, you still wouldn't have the power to get yourself into many of the auditions. It really doesn't do you much good to get a bit of information about a casting call if you don't have an agent who can get you in the door. (See Chapter 5 for details.)

In Hollywood, people who proudly say they don't have an agent and are "freelancing" are telling you one of two things: They really mean either they can't get an agent, or they're too naive to know they need one. They are making a grave mistake and their future will eventually show them how foolish they've been.

This chapter will inform you whom to contact for representation. You must be careful to get a legitimate agent. Many people move to the big city to become actors and, unfortunately, many of these newcomers will be ripped off by my con-artist friends. The problem is that when people first get to the big city they're so star-struck they'll fall for almost any scheme. "What's a couple hundred bucks to make me a star?" they think. If it were that easy, everyone and their grandmother would be a star. With the information that follows, you will learn helpful steps to take in your search, and, at the very least, how to avoid throwing your money away on doomed-to-fail methods.

ANY AGENT WHO TRIES TO SEPARATE YOU FROM YOUR MONEY BEFORE YOU LAND A JOB—ISN'T LEGIT. By legit, I'm referring to accepted practices in the professional acting industry. A legitimate agent won't get any money until *you* do—and when that happens, he'll get a percentage of your earnings, not a flat fee. If someone asks you for money up front, put your hand over your pocket, hold your wallet or purse very tightly, and run like hell.

You'll read all kinds of ads in the newspapers about companies calling themselves video casting services or some other similar name, that promise to put you on videotape to show to the studios. Unfortunately few of these tapes, if any, will ever make it to any studio. Casting directors don't have time to see tapes from casting companies that charge actors to make tapes.

When I was studying theatre at California State University in Northridge, one of my classmates announced to the class that he had just made a videotape that was going to be sent to the studios. The company that made the tape—a few-dollars cost to them—"only charged" him $500 for their services. He was excited because he thought that Universal Studios would be calling him up any day. To his knowledge the tape has never been shown, except on his own Betamax at home.

My experience, and that of other actors I know, suggests that anyone who promises to get you work as an actor is either naive or is trying to rip you off, probably the latter. No legit agent will *promise* you the landing of a job.

Determining Which Agents to Contact

ANY AGENT WHO ISN'T FRANCHISED by the union which represents the particular field you want to pursue ISN'T LEGIT. "Franchised" means that the agent has signed documents filed with the union stating that he'll abide by the rules of the union. These rules are to protect you the actor. The rules include percentages that an agent can legally take from your wages, agreements between you and the agent as to how long you'll work together, what the agent's obligation is to you, and what your obligation is to that agent, all of which are covered more fully later in this chapter and in Chapter 5.

If you're going into stage work, you want an agent who is franchised by Equity. If your career is headed in the direction of TV, film, and commercials, you want an agent who is franchised by SAG and AFTRA. You can obtain lists of franchised agents from the appropriate unions either by mail or in person. (For addresses of union offices, see Appendix A.) Most of the agents franchised by SAG are also franchised by AFTRA, so to avoid duplication, you might want to "kill two birds with one stone" and pick up the SAG list to cover both unions. The lists of agents from SAG and Equity are free to members of those respective unions, but will cost a non-member a small fee (less than a dollar) for each union list.

If you're about to do business with an agent who isn't on the appropriate list, then call the union which has jurisdiction over your particular field and check that agent out! The lists of agents include the agent's name, office address, and telephone number. In the smaller cities outside of New York and Los Angeles, you might as well submit your picture and resume to all the agents in the city where you plan to work. However, if you're working in New York or Los Angeles, submitting your picture and resume to every agent is costly, though you might end up doing this. You might want to check around with other actors in New York and Los Angeles to get an idea as to which agents are generally open to seeing new people, and which agents cater to your "type."

Another way to check out what "types" certain agents cater to, is to look through the *Academy Players Directory* if you're in Los Angeles and the *Players Guide* if you're in New York. You can obtain a copy of the *Academy Players Directory* at the Academy of Motion Picture Arts and Sciences located at 8949 Wilshire Boulevard in Beverly Hills. Information about the *Players Guide* can be obtained from any Equity office, or from the publisher at 165 West 46th Street in New York.

For a small fee an actor can have his name and picture, along with the name of his agent, printed in these publications. Many casting directors and producers refer to these manuals, so once you have an agent, it's important for you to list with these publications, if you're in New York or Los Angeles. Outside of these two areas, most theatrical and commercial agents have a "head sheet," a booklet of pictures of their clients.

Contacting the Agents

Once you've decided which agents you want to contact, this doesn't mean you should just call an agent on the phone or drop by for coffee. If you do call an agent up on the phone out of the clear blue, that agent is only going to tell you to send him a picture and resume. What have you done? You've wasted his time and your time, and you haven't made the best first impression.

The most common way to contact an agent is to mail your stapled picture and resume, accompanied by a cover letter, to the agent's office. If you send in your picture and resume without a cover letter, it appears as though you're sending mass mailings to all the agents, though in reality there's nothing wrong with doing this. The cover letter just gives it more of a personal touch. The letter should be short and to the point because agents are very busy people. If you have some film on yourself, mention that in the cover letter. (A sample cover letter is presented on the following page.)

Now you have a nice little package of material all about you—photograph, resume, and cover letter. Mail your package in an envelope large enough to avoid folding your material. Usually a nine-by-twelve inch envelope is sufficient.

After you send your package to agents, phone them if they don't call you within a week or so. They probably aren't interested if they don't call you within that time, but sometimes agents get very busy and forget to call you, or you're just not on their priority list that week. When you call an agent, simply identify yourself and explain to whomever you get on the phone that you sent your picture and resume to them on such-and-such a date. You'll probably get a secretary on the line and you might not get any further than that. But you're going to keep trying.

If none of the agents respond to your picture and resume, then your career is following the same pattern as just about everyone else's. Don't let it bother you. You can approach these same people more than once. DON'T GET DISCOURAGED! I know of very few actors who obtained an agent within a few months after moving to Los Angeles or New York. If on the first try you don't succeed, go through the list again a few months later. The agents probably won't remember your first attempt; their own situations may have changed, and they may give you a more favorable response.

Why send so many photographs and resumes to the same agents over a period of time? Because situations change—both yours and

EXHIBIT 9: Sample of Resume Cover Letter

```
                              Bill Ray
                        1111 South Street
                        Anywhere, CA 99999

                                        [date]

    Mr. Joe Smith
    Joe Smith Agency
    2000 Some Street
    Hollywood, CA 90000

    Dear Mr. Smith:

        I am interested in representation with your agency.  My most
    recent acting credit was with the Performing Arts Center in Miami.
    I played Fyedka in "Fiddler on the Roof."

        Thank you very much for taking the time to look over my enclosed
    photo and resume.  I hope to hear from you soon.

                                        Sincerely,


                                        Bill Ray


    Enclosures:  head shot and resume
```

the agents'. For example, many agents take clients by physical "type" which we've been talking about in previous chapters. In other words, agents want so many all-American types, so many street kid types, so many prostitute types, and so on. Maybe when you sent your first package to a particular agent, he already had plenty of clients that fit your type. But eventually he might receive your package at a time when he could use someone like you.

A struggling performer friend of mine named Alice kept sending pictures and resumes to agents and each of them told her they weren't looking for a "blonde bomb-shell," which is her type. This went on for a period of about a year, and finally an agent she was contacting happened to be low on the beautiful sexy types, and agreed to see Alice on an interview. The agent took her on as a client. Alice obtained an agent because of one special trait she has that all successful actors have—PERSISTANCE.

Agents will turn down actors for other reasons as well. Sometimes an agent won't take you on as a client because your credits might not be up to his standards. An agent may not handle you because you're not a member of a union. Or an agent may simply be too busy; he may be representing established actors with household names. Trying to get a newcomer in the door would probably consume more of his time than it would be worth. After all, agents are in the business to make money.

A "big" agent is one who handles established actors and who has more clout with the producers. Generally "big" is in no reference to how many clients the agent actually handles. If you're being handled by the same agent who handles Robert Redford, then you'll have a much better chance of getting interviewed for a Robert Redford movie than if you were with a smaller agent. The more stars an agent handles, the more pull he has.

However, an agent handling Robert Redford will probably work harder for Redford than for yourself. When you're first starting out in New York or Los Angeles, it's sometimes better to be handled by a "smaller" agent. The smaller agent can't sit around relying on his star clients to pay his rent. He has to rely on people like yourself.

Once you start chatting with other actors and you learn more and more about the business, you'll begin to know who handles whom. As for the smaller cities, it's unlikely that any agent will be handling a stable of stars. You can check with other actors in your city to get an idea as to which agents seem to be doing more work than others.

The Importance and Role of the Acting Unions

Earlier in this chapter, I told you you would need an agent who is franchised by the appropriate union. There are *good* reasons for this. The legit studios do not negotiate with agents who aren't franchised by the screen unions. Likewise, professional theatre producers do not negotiate with non-Equity agents.

Another reason for your need for a franchised agent is the fact that franchised agents make their money by getting you work. It is to their advantage to work hard for you. The non-franchised agent usually makes his money from charging actors to sign up with him. Why does this non-franchised agent need to get work for his clients? He's making a fortune just "signing up" actors.

You are protected by the unions when dealing with franchised agents. If you have a grievance to take up with one of these agents over any matters, you can contact the appropriate union, and its staff will help you and the agent resolve the matter. Likewise, a franchised agent is your representative with employers. If you have any differences with the company you're working for, the company will consult your agent instead of you. The franchised agent can contact the appropriate union, and along with the employer, work out the differences; whereas the non-franchised agent doesn't have this bargaining power with the unions standing behind him.

A good example concerns the time I was working on a film in Big Bear, California, a resort town in the San Bernardino Mountains, when a dispute erupted between the production company and myself. I was informed on July 3rd that I would have to shoot on July 4th, though I would not be paid extra for working on the holiday; this is against SAG rules. I had very little to say in the matter; after all, I was way up in the mountains and it was me against the production company. I called my agent, who in turn contacted a representative at SAG, and the matter was settled very quickly.

It's important that you become a member of the appropriate acting union(s). You're considered a professional actor only after you become a member of a professional acting union.

Anyone can join AFTRA. All you have to do is come up with the initiation fee. If you have the money and don't mind spending it, you might consider joining AFTRA if the screen is the area of acting you're interested in. You'll eventually have to join AFTRA anyway if you do any live or taped TV shows.

Since anyone can join AFTRA, however, it doesn't carry anywhere near as much weight as being a member of SAG carries, for getting an agent. SAG is the union you should be most concerned about if you're interested in the screen. If you're a member of AFTRA and have spoken a line of dialogue under an AFTRA contract, you would be eligible to join SAG one year after you were cast in the role where you spoke that line. In other words, if you just went down to AFTRA and paid your money to join, that wouldn't fulfill the eligibility requirement for joining SAG through AFTRA. (Specific eligibility requirements for joining SAG are reprinted in Appendix B.)

If you're a member of SAG, then screen agents know that you've worked professionally in front of the motion picture or TV camera. Working in front of the camera is much different from working on the stage. Also, since most producers are reluctant to see you for interviews if you aren't a member of SAG, it would stand to reason that most agents will be reluctant to take you on as a client. Similarly, many stage agents won't take you on if you're not a member of Equity. To join Equity, you must first obtain a role or stage manager's position in an Equity stage production, or become a member of the Equity Membership Candidate Program. (Details of the Equity Membership Candidate Program, and the specific eligibility requirements for joining AEA, are reprinted in Appendix C.)

On Union Affiliation

Your primary concern as an actor is with SAG, AFTRA, and Equity, discussed above. But it might be useful for you to get a quick overview of all the performers unions before you start searching for an agent. Having that information may protect you from going to the wrong person for the wrong thing, and from asking what may seem like amateurish questions. There are five performers' unions that make up the Associated Actors and Artists of America (or "4A's")—SAG, AFTRA, Equity, AGVA, and AGMA. Each of those, as well as SEG, is briefly sketched below. (Note: If you're a member of any of the 4A's, or SEG, and you join another 4A union, the initiation fee and dues stated below will be substantially less, in most cases one-half.) All figures below are subject to change.

• Screen Actors Guild (SAG) is the union having jurisdiction over performers working in feature films, filmed TV shows, filmed commercials, and industrial films. One can become a member by being cast in a filmed union production, TV or otherwise, as a speaking player, or as a stunt player even if he doesn't speak. *Under certain conditions* members of any other 4A union, or SEG, may also join. In commercial acting, one may be eligible to join even without speaking a line. (See Chapter 7 for details.) The initiation fee for joining SAG is $600, plus $37.50 for the first six months' dues; total joining fee is $637.50. In order to fully understand all the technical "ins and outs" of membership into SAG, you might want to pick up a copy of the "Complete Basic Agreement" from any SAG office. Though it's free for members, there is a $1.75 charge for non-members. (See specific eligibility requirements for joining SAG, in Appendix B.)

• American Federation of Television and Radio Artists (AFTRA) has jurisdiction over performers working in live and taped TV shows, taped commercials and industrials, radio shows, and phonograph records. The only requirement for joining AFTRA is that you pay its initiation fee and dues; the amounts vary from one office to another. In Los Angeles, the initiation fee is $300, plus $22 for the first six months' dues; total joining fee being $322. In New York the initiation fee is $300, plus $23.75 for the first six months' dues; total joining fee being $323.75.

● Actors Equity Association (AEA or Equity) is the union having jurisdiction over performers and stage managers in play productions. The most common way to become eligible to join Equity is by being cast, or obtaining a stage manager's position, in an Equity stage production. One can also become a member by joining the Equity Membership Candidate Program at a participating Equity theatre. (See specific eligibility requirements for joining AEA, in Appendix C.) The initiation fee for joining is $500, plus $26 for the first six months' dues; total joining fee being $526.

● Screen Extras Guild (SEG) is the union having jurisdiction over extras in feature films, filmed TV shows, and filmed commercials, in a locale which has a SEG office—Los Angeles, San Francisco, San Diego, Las Vegas, and Hawaii. Eligibility requirements for joining SEG include obtaining a job as an extra on a union show. First the performer registers with a union casting office in a city which has a SEG office. Check with the union to obtain the names of these casting offices. If that casting office is able to use you in a production, it will request SEG to allow you to become a member. You are then sent BY THAT CASTING OFFICE to SEG to join. The initiation fee is $400, plus $36 for the first six months' dues; total joining fee being $436.

● American Guild of Variety Artists (AGVA) is the union having jurisdiction over a wide variety of LIVE performers, ranging from circus clowns to night club performers. The only requirement for joining is that you are a working performer, or a member of another 4A union, and can pay the initiation fee of $300, plus your first six months' dues (which varies depending on your first contract). If you don't already have a contract when you join, your first six months' dues will be $21.

● American Guild of Musical Artists (AGMA) is the union having jurisdiction over opera singers, classical dancers, and choral singers. To join you must be employed by an AGMA employer, or already be a member of another 4A union. The initiation fee is on a sliding scale from $100 up to a maximum of $400, depending on the performer's income within AGMA's jurisdiction. Dues range from a minimum of $38, up to a maximim of $492 per year.

You do not have to join a union immediately after you obtain a job. You can "Taft-Hartley" your first job; "Taft-Hartley" is a law stating that you can work a certain amount of time on a union job without having to join that union. Some of the unions interpret this law differently, but as it typically applies to the acting unions, you can work up to thirty calendar days on your first job without joining the unions. However, on your second job, or any job that you obtain after thirty calendar days, or any job that continues over thirty calendar days, you must join if you want to work on a union show under that particular union. (This law does not apply to right-to-work states because a union cannot enforce the joining of that union in those states.)

There have been discussions about a possible merger of SAG, AFTRA, and SEG, but as of this printing, no such merger has taken place.

Okay, so now that you know the basic requirements for union affiliation, you may be dismayed. You discover that you can't get the union credentials you need without having a job first—and the agents are reluctant to help you *find* a job if you're not a member of the appropriate union. But the situation is not desperate. Both (1) your performance in showcase plays and (2) film on yourself, for example, can be helpful.

Performing in Showcase Plays

No matter what your emphasis is, you should get into some plays that are being performed in the town in which you plan to work as an actor. The picture-resume routine might not work for you and many agents do get out to see the plays.

Agents most frequently attend "showcase" plays. Those are

plays that are being performed to "showcase" the actor, writer, or director. The most common type of showcase plays in Los Angeles are called Equity Waiver plays, and in New York they're called Off-Off Broadway plays. Equity Waiver (Los Angeles) and Showcase Code (agreement which has jurisdiction over the Off-Off Broadway plays in New York) serve the same purpose, though the technical contents of the agreements differ. Both of these types of plays, though there are five variations of the Showcase Code, are staged in theatres of "99 seats or less," and are produced specifically to help new artists showcase their respective talents. For this reason, though the play is under Equity rules, the actors are rarely paid. (Acting in these plays does *not* fulfill the eligibility requirement for joining Equity.) Equity members may also audition and perform in these showcase plays.

Another type of showcase play is the "non-Equity" production. Any play that isn't under the jurisdiction of Equity is a non-Equity play. Equity members may not perform in such plays. Generally, less experienced actors are in the non-Equity productions, and for this reason, usually fewer agents are in the audience (as far as New York and Los Angeles are concerned). You can obtain information about showcase play auditions from "Backstage" and "Show Business" in New York, and "Drama-Logue" in Los Angeles. Many of the smaller cities don't have these professional showcase plays, but do have community and Little Theatre plays which, at least in those cities, can serve the same purpose.

Once you are cast in a showcase play, you can send notices to agents about your performance. As with your cover letter, be brief; simply invite the agent, provide the address of the theatre and the dates of the performance, and mention that you are seeking representation. (See sample notice on the following page.) Most showcase theatres will admit "industry" people (i.e., agents, producers, casting directors, etc.) for free. It's also a good idea to include your picture and resume along with the invitation, but it isn't mandatory. Only a small percentage of the agents whom you invite will actually attend the play, but that's to be expected. Remember

EXHIBIT 10: Sample of Letter Inviting Agents
to Attend Showcase Play

```
                        Bill Ray
                     1111 South Street
                     Anywhere, CA 99999

                                        [date]

Mr. Joe Smith
Joe Smith Agency
2000 Some Street
Hollywood, CA 90000

Dear Mr. Smith:

    I am inviting you to see me perform in "You're a Good Man,
Charlie Brown," being performed at the North Hollywood Little
Theatre, located at 1010 Mission Road.

    Please call the theatre at 666-6666 to get your complimentary
tickets.  The play will run September 16-25.  Curtain time is
8:30 p.m.

    Enclosed is a flyer on the play, along with my head shot and
resume.  I am seeking representation, so I hope you will come
see me perform.  Thank you very much for any consideration.

                                   Sincerely,


                                   Bill Ray


Enclosure:   flyer on play
             head shot and resume
```

that other members of the cast will also have sent out notices; this will broaden the number of agents in the audience. (Note: If you are cast in one of these plays be sure to have a plentiful supply of pictures and resumes with you—*every night of each performance.* You never know who might be in the audience; afterwards someone might ask you for your picture and resume.)

Submitting Film on Yourself

If you plan to pursue a career in TV, film, and commercials, then doing these plays is important, but it's even more important to have film on yourself, which we briefly mentioned in Chapter 3. (Keep in mind that having a videotape of yourself is referred to as "film on yourself" in everyday jargon, but should be referred to as "Tape Available" on your resume, if in fact your scene is on videotape.) Watching an actor on stage gives the screen agent some idea of the actor's ability on STAGE. However, seeing an actor on SCREEN not only shows that agent your acting ability in FRONT OF THE CAMERA, but it will also show him how you react to the camera and how well you DO or DON'T photograph.

The best film to have on yourself would be from network television or a feature film. But many actors, and especially those just getting started, don't have such film to show. One place you can get good film on yourself is from universities with strong film and TV departments. The reason I say "strong" is because you don't want a "cheapy" looking film to show to agents or casting directors. It would be better to have no film whatsoever than "bad" film.

Provided you are not a member of SAG or AFTRA, you can also get good film on yourself from "non-SAG" and "non-AFTRA" shows. These are shows that aren't shot under union jurisdiction, so they use beginners. (Non-union productions are discussed in more detail in Chapter 6.) Whatever type of film you perform in, MAKE SURE YOU HAVE DIALOGUE. Agents are not interested in seeing you in a scene in which you don't speak. In New York and

Los Angeles, you can obtain information about college productions and non-union, as well as union, productions from the trade publications we've been discussing. Most of the college film production auditions in New York and Los Angeles are open to anyone who wishes to audition. That's because in those cities there is such a talent pool to select from and even professionals like to get better film on themselves than they might presently have. In the smaller cities simply call local college film and TV departments to find out about their auditions. Some of the universities will allow student filmmakers to have open auditions, and other universities will restrict the filmmakers to auditioning only registered students at their university. You can also contact local film and video production houses and inquire about their productions. Many cities have companies which shoot educational and industrial films and tapes.

If you are cast in any type of film or taped show, be sure to get a copy of your scene(s). Then have the scene(s) transferred to ¾″ videotape, if they are presently on film. You can have this done at just about any videotape editing facility. If you are in a college film production, many of the film departments have the facilities to do this for you. One thing to keep in mind about your tape is that it should be short; five minutes is long enough (good editing is, of course, a must).

There are companies, especially in Hollywood, that for a fee will make a tape of you which you can take to the agents on your own. Generally these are a waste of time, but I guess there are exceptions. They usually look very amateurish and the agent wonders why you couldn't get into some actual university film or TV production. One must consider the agent's point of view. Why should an agent look at homemade tapes of actors who obviously haven't worked in a professional or university production, when he can view tapes of other actors in actual shooting situations?

As pointed out earlier, if you have film on yourself, it's a good idea to mention that on your resume and in your cover letter. Anytime you have an interview with an agent, take the tape with you.

You can also take the tape to various agents' offices, without an appointment. Some of the agents will see your tape (probably not at that moment) and other agents will tell you to get lost. The advantage of the tape is that screen agents can view it at their convenience. DO NOT GIVE THEM AN ORIGINAL TAPE! Have duplicates made of your original; sometimes tapes get lost in the shuffle.

The important thing here is to find a way to show the agents your abilities. No matter how talented you are, if they don't see your work, the talent is useless. Few agents will take you on without seeing some of your work first. An agent's reputation is at stake every time he sends you to an audition or interview; he'll be depending on *your* skills as an actor. An agent will have more confidence in you if he knows what you can do, and if he likes what you do, he'll work harder for you.

* * * * * * *

YOU CAN GET AN AGENT. YOU WILL GET AN AGENT, but it might not be right this minute. It is likely that every present star has been turned down by some agent. And, by the same token, many future stars are, at this minute, being turned down by agents. The important thing to keep in mind is that you need to keep your head up. The odds will be in your favor if you keep sending out pictures and resumes to the agents, continue trying to get some good film on yourself, and keep acting in plays around town and inviting those agents to come see you perform. Eventually all the preparatory work you have done will pay off—you will obtain an interview with an agent. How to handle that interview, as well as other aspects of DEALING WITH AGENTS, is discussed in the next chapter.

Chapter 5

DEALING WITH
THE AGENT

What should you do to make a good impression on the agent? How should *you* choose your agent as well as be chosen by one? What should you expect from a contract? How do you get out of an unsatisfactory one? How many agents can you or should you have? What is *your* role in working with an agent? Should you have a manager? By the time you complete reading this chapter, you should be able to answer these questions and be able to handle your interview(s) professionally—and successfully.

Going For the Interview

First of all, BE ON TIME for the interview. Being late only tells the agent that you're not a very responsible person and that you're not taking your career very seriously.

DRESS CASUALLY for the interview. Men don't need to wear coats and ties, and women don't need to wear high-fashion dresses. Dressing in clothes that cost more money than it would take to feed the population of China is a no-no. Also, don't wear heavy make-up.

Back in the early days of film, much acting was very stylized. The actors had just come from the stage where everything—make-up, gestures, facial expressions, etc.—is played much broader. Even the stars of the early days were of the glamorous type. But look at your stars of today—most of them are more "natural" looking.

On the other hand, don't be sloppy. If you look as though you could walk into a rummage sale and get sold, then you're probably underdressed. The best policy is to go in between. Nice jeans/slacks and shirt are pretty standard. As with your photographs, you want to keep the attention on your face. For example, women shouldn't wear clothes that are physically distracting. Clothes that would embarrass the family doctor are a no-no. (You *can* consider dressing sexily for an interview if you think that's the kind of role you'll be auditioning for. Even then, however, be subtle about it.)

BRING PICTURES AND RESUMES to the interview. Bring your head shot, plus the proof sheets from the original shooting that you selected your head shot from, if you have them. If you had a few eight-by-tens printed before you decided which one you actually wanted to use for your head shot, bring them also; the extra photos will give the agent a better idea of how you photograph. (Note: It isn't mandatory to have the proof sheets and extra photos.)

HAVE A COUPLE OF SHORT MONOLOGUES PRE-PARED if you're going to have an interview with a stage agent. You should prepare both a serious and a humorous monologue, each between three and five minutes long. Most stage agents would rather see you perform on stage (see discussion of showcase plays in Chapter 4), but have the monologues prepared, just in case. It's a good idea to prepare a short monologue, preferably something light and humorous, if you're going to have an interview with a screen agent, though few of them will actually want to see you perform one—better to be safe than sorry. Usually if the screen agent wants you to bring in prepared material, however, he'll notify you in advance of the interview, and he would most likely want you to bring in a two-person scene. In that case, you'd be expected to show up at the interview with another actor. Keep in mind that the interview is for YOU, so be sure to pick a scene that will show YOU off rather than your partner. The two-person scene gives the agent a better idea of how natural you can be when you're working close-up with another actor, which is very important for screen acting. The scene should, like the monologue for screen agents, be light and humorous. Shakespeare's material doesn't give the screen agent much knowledge of how natural you are with dialogue.

BE MENTALLY PREPARED FOR A "COLD READING" if you're going to have an interview with a TV, film, or commercial agent. Giving a "cold reading" means that you'll be reading material with little preparation, if any. The agent will probably have you look over the material for a few minutes and then ask you to perform it. Unless the material is very short, most agents won't ask you to memorize it on the spot.

The reason for this cold reading is that most roles for TV shows, films, and commercials are cast only a few days before the actual shooting. Roles for regulars in TV series (roles that are on every episode) and the starring roles in films can take longer, but they too are sometimes cast within a few days of the actual shooting. On many occasions producers will start shooting a film or a particular episode of a TV show even before all the roles have been cast; producers will cast the actors they need for the first few days of shooting, and then cast the others as they get to them in the script. In episodic TV (weekly series shows) the producers sometimes cast on the day that comes in between the shooting of each episode! In soap opera work, roles are cast as they crop up; the scripts are only a few days ahead of each day's shooting. Likewise, commercials are cast and shot within a matter of days.

The first episodic prime-time TV show I was cast in was called "Project UFO" for NBC. I was cast late one Thursday afternoon. When I arrived back at my house after the interview, I had a message from my agent informing me that I got the part and was to shoot the next day, Friday. Friday was actually the last shooting day for that particular episode of the show. I had to immediately rush over to the wardrobe department at Samuel Goldwyn Studios. The script was sent to my house by messenger late that Thursday night. I spent most of the evening learning lines, and at six the next morning I was out at the location in Malibu. At the time I thought this mad rush was unusual, but as I began to work on more shows I came to realize that this is the norm.

Since time is money in TV and film, producers don't have time to send the scripts out to all the actors who will be interviewed for the show. Also, ideas are easily stolen, and TV and film producers don't like to have their scripts floating around town. Thus, almost all screen interviews will include a cold reading. So it stands to reason that a screen agent would want to know your cold reading capabilities before taking you on as a client.

Conversely, many stage agents won't have you perform a cold reading, if they don't handle actors for TV and film. Unless it is original and being performed for the first time, a play can usually be checked out of a library or purchased from a drama book store; if the play is an original one, often your agent can get a copy of it to you before the audition. So the stage actor usually knows the material in the play before he auditions. Therefore, the cold reading is less used for stage auditions—but be mentally prepared for one anyway.

SHOW THE AGENT THAT YOU HAVE A PLEASING PERSONALITY. The agent will chat with you to get a general feeling about you. If you're nervous, you might find yourself either giving one- or two-word answers, or, in the other direction, going on and on saying nothing of significance or *interest.* Try to catch your breath, and avoid both of these extremes. The idea is to get the agent interested in you . . . so don't bore him! If the interviewer has seen better conversations in his alphabet soup, he probably won't be very impressed. After all, this is a "personality" business.

You can establish some commonality of interest by a simple technique: Look around his office and see what types of things he likes. A person's office often reflects his personality. Are there pictures of cats on the walls? Are there plants hanging all over the place? Is the interviewer a family-type person—are there family pictures on his desk?

At some point, the agent will probably ask you something like, "What have you been doing lately?" An answer such as "About what?" isn't appropriate. Your answer should include what you've been doing in the area of acting. After all, that's where the agent's interest in you lies. He is also getting an idea of your personality, so try to also tell him some other interesting things. For example, you might tell him some funny episodes that have happened in your search for an agent, etc. Agents and casting directors generally love show-biz stories. But keep the stories short; you don't want an agent to have a hard time getting you out of his office.

The agent might ask you whom you're studying with, or have studied with, even though it should appear on your resume. If you're studying with someone in the same town as the agent, he will probably know something about your teacher. He might even have enough of a rapport with your teacher to call him up on the phone to see how you're doing. Remember, though, whom you're studying with won't carry as much weight as having CREDITS. Schooling is only a means to an end. I seriously doubt any acting school will impress an agent as much as your acting jobs. College degrees just really aren't important to them, though the degree is important to the actor, if he received experience on the college stage. If you were hiring someone to build you a house, for example, would you rather hire someone who'd just finished contracting school, or someone who had actually built many homes? If you have a heavy credit list, then the agent probably won't even ask whom you've been studying with. However, if you have only a few credits, or none whatsoever, the answer to this question could take on SOME importance.

KEEP A POSITIVE ATTITUDE during the interview. The interview should be very "up." The agent doesn't want to hear depressing stories about what a hard time you're having getting started in the acting profession. Don't develop what I like to call "actor's syndrome." This refers to the depressed actor that nobody wants. It's the same as in dating: If you were dating someone who kept telling you (verbally and otherwise) that no one wanted him, you'd begin to realize why!

DEPART IN POLITE AND TIMELY FASHION. Granted that you want to stay in the agent's office as long as you can—the longer you're in there, the better chance he has of remembering you. *But,* agents are very busy people, and the law of diminishing returns takes effect if you overstay your welcome. When the interview starts to die down, don't go on and on about just anything. Simply get ready to depart. And if the interviewer was ruder than your in-laws, you still want to leave on a positive note. Shake his hand, look him right in the eye, smile, thank him, and get out!

Contracts

If an agent wants to represent you, he might have you sign a contract, either on the spot or a few days later. I've stressed in this book that you sign a contract only with an AGENT WHO IS ON THE LEGIT UNION'S AGENCY LIST for your particular field. If you stick with that, you are protected from being ripped off. The contracts you'll sign with franchised agents are standard within each respective union.

There's nothing wrong with taking the contracts home and reading them over, however, if they give you the contract right then and there to sign. As a matter of fact, if you've never read one, then it just makes good sense to read it over very carefully. If you have any questions about your contract, you can contact SAG, AFTRA, or Equity respectively, to get reliable answers.

When you sign contracts, you'll sign three copies of each: one for the agent, one for you, and one for the appropriate union. The advantage of the union having a copy is that the union will know who your representative is. Sometimes producers call the union to find out how they can get in touch with a certain actor. If you have signed contracts with an agent, the union will be able to inform any producer who your representative is, should he need your services.

The contract you sign with a "legit" agent guarantees that he'll make a percentage of your salary. The maximum an agent can take

---

A Few Pointers About Managers

You've read all the stories about the managers of big stars, and you've seen those magazine photos of them standing together. So you decide that if you just had a manager, you too could reach stardom and big money. Well, if you're just starting out, I wouldn't suggest going the manager route—you probably aren't familiar enough with them to evaluate who is legit and who isn't; and there are no unions protecting you, as there are with agents.

But, if you're determined—or approached—at least keep these pointers in mind:

● The manager's job is to manage your career. The manager will help you change agents when you need to. He will keep on top of your agent to make sure he is adequately representing you. The manager also solicits work for actors, much in the same way an agent does. The advantage of a manager is that you'll have more people working in your behalf.

● As with agents, any manager who charges you money up-front isn't legit. Managers usually take around fifteen percent of

---

from your salary is ten percent, which is standard. (There are *extremely rare* cases in which a star has negotiated a five percent take with an agent.)

Sometimes your employer will send your check(s) directly to you, but your agent still will know what you are being paid for each job. If he negotiated the contract, he'll obviously know what his and your cut should be. If you negotiated the contract yourself, all the agent has to do is check with the casting director of that particular show or contact the union to find out what you made on the particular job. The contract also states that no matter *who* gets you the job, and no matter who negotiates the contract, the agent is *still* entitled to his percentage. Most often the check will be mailed directly to your agent. By the time you get your first job, your agent an actor's salary. There are no regulations regarding this, however; they can take as much as they can get.

● Since managers aren't franchised by the unions, they can't legally negotiate contracts with employers, though frankly many of them do through a third party—agent, the actor himself, or an attorney—all who can legally negotiate a contract. Many managers have personal friends who are directors, producers, network executives, etc. A *good manager* wants an actor's career that he can manage; therefore he usually isn't interested in newcomers. WHETHER OR NOT YOU HAVE A MAN-AGER, YOU STILL NEED AN AGENT (whose ten percent is *not* included in the cut the manager takes).

● A good manager handles only around ten clients, whereas an agent handles maybe a hundred, or more. There are a very few good managers, ones who have terrific connections and can do wonders for your career. There are a great many managers who can't do anything for your career. FIRST get an agent, and LATER worry about a manager if you think your career needs a little guidance.

probably would've had you sign check authorizations; in other words, the authorizations give him permission to cash your checks from any acting employment. It's standard for an agent to do this; don't let it throw you. When an agent receives your check from a production company, he'll cash it at his bank, and write you a check for your ninety percent of the original amount.

At this point, you might be wondering how you can protect yourself from being ripped off by your agent. First of all, as is the case with your agent, you'll know how much money you're making on the show, so you'll know exactly what you and your agent's cut will be. Second, your agent will mail your statement of earnings from your employer with your check. Third, as stated earlier, the union has a record of how much you made on the job; you can call its office if you have any problems. Fourth, you'll get your W-2 forms at the end of the year, stating your earnings. Quite frankly, I cannot imagine any franchised agent trying to rip you off. His entire business is at stake if he gets caught doing such a thing; he could be defranchised by the appropriate union, and there are too many ways for him to get caught.

The contracts you'll sign with agents are separate for each union. Be comforted to know that there are escape clauses in each of the contracts you sign with legit agents.

The agent has an easy way out of a contract with an actor; he just stops submitting the actor for interviews/auditions, and eventually the actor will move on to another agent. The actor who wants to release an agent, however, must adhere to certain provisions, which are stated below. The same escape clauses apply no matter what the duration of the actor's contract happens to be. If you want to leave an agent and you fall into any of the situations below, you simply send a registered letter to the agent informing him of your departure, and also send a copy of the letter to the appropriate union.

SAG—For filmed TV and film contracts, if you've worked fewer than 15 days in the last 91, or have had no work in the last 77 days, you can release yourself from the contract. For commercial contracts, if you signed an *original* contract and you haven't made $2,000 or more in commercials in a period of 151 days, or not had a "bona fide offer" for employment in the last 121 days, you can terminate the contract. ("Bona fide offer" means that the agent has secured an actual acting job for you, contract and all, not just, for example, a submission of your photo and resume.) If you've signed a *renewal* commercial contract and you haven't made $2,000 or more in the last 91 days, you can release yourself from the contract. Your *original* SAG contract with any particular agent can only be signed up to a maximum of one year. You can renew the contract at the end of that time for a period of up to three years, if you're satisfied with the agent. And if that agent is not satisfied with you, then you would not want him to represent you longer than that anyway. After all, if an agent isn't excited about you, that agent definitely won't put much effort into furthering your career.

AFTRA—For the commercial and TV contract, if you worked fewer than 15 days in the last 91, you can release yourself from the contract. AFTRA contracts can be signed up to a maximum of three years.

EQUITY—If you haven't had a bona fide offer of employment in the last 90 days, you can terminate the contract. The initial contract can be signed for a maximum of eighteen months. The second contract, with that same agent, can be signed up to a maximum of three years.

One Agent or More?

You CAN have DIFFERENT agents for DIFFERENT fields, EVEN if you sign CONTRACTS with all of them. In other words, you can have a commercial agent, a TV and film agent, and a stage agent. Many agencies have a separate department for each field. If an agent represents you for more than one area, you can release yourself from one of the areas and retain him for the others, if you're not happy with him in a particular area. Of course this can become "touchy." You have to use your own judgment about whether or not to leave an agent for a particular field while retaining him for others.

IT IS AGAINST ALL UNION RULES TO SIGN A CONTRACT WITH MORE THAN ONE AGENT AT A TIME FOR A PARTICULAR FIELD. In other words, you can't sign a theatrical contract (TV and film) with two agents or sign a stage contract with more than one agent. Obviously, having signed with two agents for the same field creates a confusing situation for the casting directors—and could present you with "interesting" legal questions. Who would be your representative? To whom would you pay your ten percent? If you've signed two contracts stating that you'll pay ten percent to each agent and you get a job, you now owe twenty percent and it's against all union rules to pay more than ten percent in agent fees; if found out you could be brought up on charges by the union.

Many times you won't have to sign a contract with an agent who's working on your behalf, at the beginning. He'll agree to work for you and might wait until you get your first job before signing anything. It's basically to your advantage to sign a union contract with a franchised agent; usually it means that the agent is more interested in you if he goes through the paperwork of signing you up. However, if he doesn't sign you right away, this doesn't mean he *isn't* interested in you.

Once you get your first job, the agent still doesn't *have* to sign contracts with you, though if he has not already, this is usually the time that he does. If you don't sign a contract even after you obtain employment, you are *still* obligated to give your agent his ten percent, *if he negotiated the deal.* You have a *verbal* contract with that agent when you agree to work together, and the unions expect you to stand by that agreement. The agent could bring you up on charges with the respective union if you fall back on your part of the deal.

In Hollywood, it's considered in bad taste to work under more than one agent for the same field even if you don't sign contracts. It confuses the casting directors as to whom your representative is and in the end you'll be the one losing out; the casting director doesn't want to call one agent to negotiate without talking to the other, because he doesn't want that other agent on his back. Conclusion: IN HOLLYWOOD DON'T HAVE TWO AGENTS FOR THE SAME FIELD, EVEN IF NO CONTRACTS HAVE BEEN SIGNED!

In New York, on the other hand, it is pretty standard for an actor to work under different agencies even for the same field, without a signed contract. Whichever agent gets you in the door, gets the ten percent if you land the job. Remember, though, this applies *only* if you don't have a signed contract. In New York the casting directors are aware that actors may be working under more than one agent for the same field, and it doesn't seem to bother them.

As pointed out earlier, some agents handle all areas, some a combination of areas, and others only one area. Some actors *prefer* to have one agency represent them exclusively. The advantage to this is that all your business transactions will be going through one office; the disadvantage is that very few agents are strong in all fields. To that disadvantage, some actors choose to sign with a large agent who *specializes* in the field of the actor's strongest interest, but who has other departments as well. Many actors who are just starting out will end up with a smaller agent who is a kind of jack-of-all-trades—representing all areas, but not specializing in any particular one.

Shuffling agents can be tricky. Suppose you get signed by a terrific commerical agent. Then you start looking for a theatrical agent. Let's suppose you find a theatrical agent who also happens to represent actors commercially and he wants you for both areas. But suppose this new agent isn't as good a commercial agent as the commercial agent you already have. What do you do? You want the theatrical agent, but you also want the terrific commercial agent. There are no clear-cut answers to such situations. You'll just have to look at the situation from all angles and make your decisions should you end up in this situation. However, most agents, if they really want you, will take you as a client in one area without necessarily representing you in other areas, if this is your wish.

Actor/Agent Relationships

On occasion you'll hear actors talk badly about their agents. "The last interview my agent sent me on was for 'Gone With The Wind.'" "The last time I had an interview I believe sound had just come into the movies." Some comments like these could be warranted. Some agents and actors just don't work well together, just as some psychiatrists and patients have problems working together. That first year, at least, is definitely a trial and error period for both of you.

But be careful about sitting around talking about how bad luck has caught up with you with the agent you have. Thinking that

Karma is getting even with you because you played "I'll show you mine, if you'll show me yours" with a former classmate in the third grade is destructive. Instead of complaining about your agent, simply call him up on the phone every once in a while and ask him why you're not going out on interviews and auditions. Keep on your agent's back, but DON'T BE A PEST!

In the meantime, do a lot of hustling on your own. An agent has many careers to look after, and you have ONLY ONE. This will not interfere with the work your agent is doing for you. Many actors will tell you that they get a lot of work on their own, though they still need an agent for business reasons, which we've already discussed. Send pictures and resumes to casting directors, and phone them to see if you can set up "general interviews" in which you just go into their offices and chat. A general interview isn't as important as an interview for a particular part; however, when your picture and resume are submitted to that casting director in the future, by you or your agent, you may have a better chance of getting into the interview because the casting director knows you.

Audition for plays around town that will showcase your talent. (See Chapter 4 for more information on showcase plays.) Read the trade publications to get an idea what is being cast and what is being shot. Taking the initiative like this will aid your career, and will enhance the work your agent is doing for you.

Keep in mind that just because you aren't going on interviews and auditions, doesn't necessarily mean that your agent isn't working for you. Even if you have lots of credits and are a member of the acting unions, it's still hard to get in the doors to see casting directors. Your agent isn't the only agent out there trying to accomplish this task.

Let me point out that few actors obtain work in the first few months after signing a contract with an agent. I would suggest that you stick it out with your agent for awhile before releasing him from your contract. In the course of one year if you haven't been going out on very many auditions then you can re-evaluate. Base your decision of whether to stick with that agent on how many interviews and auditions he's gotten you into in a year's time. There are really no guidelines or statistics to show how many times you should go out in the course of a year. It's generally much less, however, than people would imagine. Check with other actors who are your "type" to see how much they've been going out. But you have to keep in mind that just because they might be going out more than you, that doesn't necessarily mean you should be going out as much. What about their credit lists? Have they been in the business longer than you? Consider all the possibilities before condemning your agent.

If you decide to leave your agent, DON'T break off relations yet. Find another agent first. Start sending out pictures and resumes to other agents and see what responses you get. You might find that no other agent wants to take you on as a client at that moment; in that case you would at least still have your old agent to represent you. If you aren't already convinced that having an agent is crucial to the development of your acting career, then you will be after you read the next chapter, on HOW ROLES ARE CAST.

Chapter 6

HOW ROLES ARE CAST IN THE BIG TIME

If you want to do stage work, then New York is where the main action is. If you want to do TV and film work, then you should "Go west, young man." (Many commercials are shot on both coasts.) This is not to say that there's no TV and film work in New York, or no stage work in Los Angeles, but New York is a theatre town, and Los Angeles is a screen town. Keeping the above in mind, when I write about the screen world, the slant is towards Los Angeles, and when I write about the theatre world, the slant is towards New York. However, the principles are about the same on both coasts in their similar areas.

TV and Film

You open your local newspaper in Omaha and notice that the Little Theatre is casting a play called, "Frisco, The City And The Cereal." After reading a description of the characters you decide you're right for the part of the mayor of San Francisco. So you stroll on down to the theater to read for the part. The competition is stiff, as there are thirty or forty other "mayors" who are also right for the part. This seems easy enough, however, because the Little Theatre is having open auditions and you'll at least get seen.

Let's say you got the part and your performance in the play was terrific. You mastered the play at the local level, and Aunt Bertha urges you to go for the big time. You got rave reviews in the local papers so you must be professional material.

You move to Hollywood or New York, but when you open the daily newspapers there, you don't see any interviews for TV and film roles. (I'd be skeptical of any casting interviews I read about in regular newspapers in New York or Los Angeles, anyway; professional acting jobs generally aren't advertised there.) This is very frustrating. Here you are in the big city and ready to go, but you don't know where to go to!

As we discussed in Chapter 4, you *can* find out about some SAG and AFTRA (and non-union) shows which are being cast, from such publications as "Backstage" and "Show Business" in New York, and from "Drama-Logue" in Los Angeles. In addition to those publications, in New York you can look through "Variety" (weekly), and in Hollywood, "Variety" (daily), and the "Hollywood Reporter" (daily). In Los Angeles' "Variety" and the "Hollywood Reporter," casting news is only listed in the publications once or twice a week, so check with their offices to find out which days.

Non-Union Productions

Non-union productions are many times cast from actors who find out about auditions from the publications cited above. In almost all cases, actors can get into non-union production interviews without the aid of an agent.

Should you bother to interview for non-SAG and non-AFTRA jobs? Non-SAG and non-AFTRA means that the company shooting the show isn't a signatory of the respective union. You, the actor, won't be protected by the unions if you're in one of these shows. If the company goes bankrupt, or has some "creative bookeeping" practices, you *might* not ever see your check. With a union production, however, if the company doesn't have a long-standing record of good payment with the union, or is a new company, it has to post a bond (i.e., money) to cover the actors' salaries, *before using the actors.*

Usually these low budget non-union productions aren't seen by very many people, but there are a few exceptions. Your interest in performing in one, however, isn't really the exposure or money, but rather the film you can obtain on yourself, as pointed out in Chapter 4. Keep in mind that with non-union productions you won't have the competition of union actors since union actors are forbidden from working in these shows.

Union agents may solicit non-union work for their non-union actors, *though they rarely do so.* The main reason a union agent would even get involved in non-union work for a client would be for the same reason you would—to get good film on the actor. (Producers sometimes request agents to send film on certain actors to the studios.) The union agent may still sign union contracts with a non-union actor, whether the agent is getting the client union or non-union work.

If you aren't a member of the screen unions, then you really have nothing to lose by participating in one of these shows as long as you are *extremely careful about any contracts you sign.* The contracts for employment with non-signatory companies aren't standard, so be sure to have an entertainment lawyer look them over.

Union Productions

Though you can find out about union interviews from the trade publications, ROLES FOR UNION TV AND FILM PRODUCTIONS ARE CAST ALMOST EXCLUSIVELY THROUGH AGENTS. Finding out about a union interview, and getting *yourself* into that interview, are two different things.

When a part is being cast for a union TV show or film, the studios generally call "Breakdown Services," a publication with offices and editions in Hollywood and New York. The studios and independent producers give the Breakdown Services the vital information about the casting—who's casting, where to get in touch with the casting director, the director's name, and the producer's name. Also, they give the Breakdown Services a description of each character, which may go something like this:

ABIGAIL: She is around seven feet tall, with black hair, and a crooked nose. Everyone at her spa thinks she is working for the Mafia. The woman playing Abigail must be a terrific hockey player. LEAD ROLE.

The Breakdown Services distributes this information to union agents, and to managers. It cannot be directly obtained by actors.

Each agent submits (by mail or in person) actors' pictures and resumes to the casting personnel. Agents like to submit actors who are physically right for the part, who have some decent credits, and who have a chance of getting in on the interview. Keep in mind that there are about 250 agencies in Hollywood, fewer in the smaller cities, of course. In Hollywood, if each agent only submitted ten actors for the role of Abigail, there would be 2,500 actors up for the role even before the interviewing began!

Also, more actors will be trying to get in on the interview other than the ones submitted by agents. Actors will be trying to get in "on the side" because they already know the casting director, director, or producer, or perhaps they heard about the interview on their own and sent their picture and resume to the casting personnel independently. Keep in mind that managers will also be submitting their clients (there will be some overlap here because those clients probably also have agents submitting them).

The point is clear. Competition for TV and film roles is immense. You can see from the examples above that agents have competition just as actors do. The more pull an agent has, the better chance he has of getting his clients into the interview.

Except in rare cases, you, the actor, have to be submitted by an agent before you have a decent chance of getting into the interview.

Even though you can submit yourself if you're lucky enough to find out about an interview, agency submissions will be considered before independent ones. In other words, you need to be liked immensely by your agent, so that he'll submit you, which gives you the maximum possibility of getting into the interview.

Next, the casting director sorts through all of these pictures and resumes, and selects, for example, around fifty or so actors to be interviewed. (The number varies from project to project, but this will give you an idea how the casting works.)

Maybe the casting director is a personal friend of your agent; this would help your chances of getting in on that interview. Maybe your agent used to date the casting director and they broke off on sour terms; this would damage your chances of getting in on that interview. This all sounds pretty petty, right? Welcome to big time TV and films. These things do happen. If you think they don't, then you should consider enrolling in the REALITY I course being taught at the local college.

The casting director will have general interviews with those fifty actors selected from the many whose pictures and resumes have been submitted. (Note: On all interviews and auditions, bring along a picture and resume, even though copies will have been submitted earlier by your agent.) Since the casting director is calling people into the interview after looking at their pictures, you can see why it's important that your pictures accurately represent you.

The interview with these fifty or so actors will be somewhat like the interview with an agent; the casting director will ask you the same general questions. Like the agent, he is trying to get an idea of your personality and "type." He may or may not have you read on this first interview; it depends on how much time he has to cast the show.

After interviewing these fifty actors, the casting director will call back, for example, around twenty. The casting director will contact the agents of these twenty actors to inform them when the call-backs will be held. Let's say you are one of the twenty to be called back. On this call-back you'll probably see the script. You'll give a cold reading of the material, during which the casting director will be looking to see how natural you are. The casting director is just looking for plain good ole conversation. He doesn't want actors to *read* to each other; he wants actors to *talk* to each other. Unfortunately many newcomers to TV and film are used to working only on the stage and therefore don't realize that TV and film acting is much more subtle. "Less is more" in the screen medium (exceptions: commercials, and, in many cases, situation comedies taped in front of live audiences).

So let's say that the casting director likes YOU and YOUR ACTING. He might call you back a second time to read for the director. Remember, everyone's job is at stake and the casting director only wants to send good people to the director. After all, that is the casting director's job. He saves the director and producer a lot of time.

Let's say the director likes YOUR PERSONALITY and YOUR ACTING. He might then decide to call you back a third time to meet the producer. (Sometimes the producer is present during the reading with the director, and sometimes casting director, director, and producer are all present during the first interview; again, it depends on how much time they have to cast the show.)

If the show is for TV, you might then be sent to the network for "Network Approval." However, most roles are cast by the director and/or producer, for TV and film roles. Sometimes the casting director alone will cast minor roles, especially for television. As pointed out earlier, all of the above usually takes place over the span of a few days, sometimes longer for the starring roles. (If they keep you on the interview for over an hour, or specifically ask you to take the script home and learn a scene, you might be entitled to compensation, provided it's for a union job and you're a member of the union. Check the union offices for information about any specific instances.)

It should be obvious by now that many people have to like YOU and YOUR TALENTS before you're cast in a TV show or film. Everyone's job rests on you—the actor. The idea that you can "fool around" with a couple of people in the entertainment industry and

MAKE A CAREER, is generally hogwash. Too much money and too many reputations are at stake when you're hired to do an acting job.

In TV, the networks certainly don't want incompetant actors, because they don't want to lose sponsors who do, after all, support TV. The sponsors themselves want competent actors because since they are sponsoring the show, they have a reputation at stake with the public. And, likewise, for film the producer has to answer to the people giving him the money to shoot the film. The people putting money into the project don't want incompetent actors because the public will decide if the backers get their money back or not.

Theatre

Just as in TV and film, the importance of casting in theatre is clear. As you know, large sums of money are invested in stage shows, and one actor "not working out" could possibly mean the closing of a show long before the break-even point.

There's good news and bad news concerning professional theatre acting over screen acting. The good news is that it's easier for the actor to get seen by theatre producers than by screen producers. Unfortunately, the good news causes the bad news; since it's easier to get seen, there will probably be more people in competition for each part. However, the most important consideration in being cast is first being *seen.*

You can get good experience working at your local Little Theatre and other non-Equity community theatres. This is one advantage of the stage over the screen for the actor. It's much harder to practice working on the screen in actual productions; the reason, of course, is that it's too expensive to have small screen productions, whereas theatre groups spring up in just about every town. If you're just starting out in the theatre, ANY WORK IS POSITIVE! ANY experience is good, be it local or professional, though as we've discussed earlier, on your resume non-professional productions carry much less weight than professional jobs. Eventually you'll want to perform in Equity productions because this is where actors get paid, and since you're reading my book, I take if for granted that you want to act and eat at the same time.

You don't necessarily have to have an agent to be seen by theatre producers if you're a member of Equity, though I would recommend one anyway. Generally, you'll have a more personal audition if you have an agent. Without an agent, you'll probably be "herded" in with the rest of the group and the audition will be somewhat like going through an assembly line. Theatre producers see so many people in such a short period of time that it's harder for them to remember you, than if you'd had a semi-private audition.

You can read about theatre casting news in the trade publications we've been discussing. These trade publications list Equity and non-Equity production casting news. Also, you can check the bulletin board at the New York Equity office to find out about auditions, if you are a *member*. Non-Equity members may phone any Equity office for general information about theatre acting. In Hollywood, in addition to the bulletin board, the Equity office has a hotline which gives information about Equity auditions to anyone who calls. (Call the Hollywood Equity office for that hotline number.)

Besides finding employment through trade publications, Equity offices, and agents, an actor can contact a national service organization in New York called Theatre Communications Group (TCG). Many stage auditions, Equity as well as non-Equity, are held there each year.

If you're moving to, or are presently residing in, New York, simply leave an eight-by-ten photo and resume at the TCG office and inquire as to when they will be having their regular general auditions, which are usually held twice a year; the number varies depending on when their casting directors have a slow period and can set up the auditions. An actor can also leave a flyer about any showcase play he's performing in; perhaps someone from TCG will be available to attend. The purpose of the general audition is so the TCG staff can see your work and perhaps, in the future, invite you to a specific audition for a specific play.

Like most general auditions for theatre work, TCG wants to see you perform two pieces—preferably one classical and one contemporary scene. Together they should *not* be over five minutes in length. If you can't do classical material, do whatever scenes you do best, but demonstrate variety.

TCG also has a bulletin board which anyone can check to see what plays are currently being cast there. However, you must actually be *invited* to audition for specific plays; the invitation is based on your performance at the regular general audition as discussed above.

There are different types of Equity productions for which you can audition, the variations too numerous (and confusing) to cite here. It is enough for now to learn the major, basic types. The basic **PRODUCTION CONTRACT** is used for theatres only having a single production, not a run of plays back-to-back. This type of contract has the highest wage minimums for actors. In order to relieve theatres of the high cost of the Production Contract, there are other types of contracts which have lower minimums. The requirements for a theatre being able to obtain lower minimums depends on several factors—size of the theatre, how many shows the theatre is performing back-to-back, how many of the same players are being used from one production to the other, etc. Many of the theatres under Equity contracts, other than the Production Contract, are affiliated with specific organizations. The organizations negotiate contracts with Equity on behalf of the theatres which are affiliated with them. The organizations and/or contracts are as follows:

LORT (League of Resident Theatres) is the negotiating body for Equity resident theatres all over the country. By Equity definition, to be considered a resident company the theatre must be producing a series of plays; in other words, the theatre isn't set up to produce only a single production. LORT theatres are non-profit organizations.

CORST & COST (Council of Resident Stock Theatres, and Council of Stock Theatres [non-resident], respectively) are the negotiating bodies for dramatic stock companies all over the country. By Equity definition, to be considered a stock company the theatre must be producing two or more plays simultaneously. Stock companies usually aren't non-profit organizations, as are LORT theatres. The main difference between CORST and COST is that CORST maintains a nucleus of performers from one play to the next.

TYA (Theatre for Young Audiences) is the contract used for plays which are being produced for children. By Equity definition, in order for a company to use the TYA contracts, the play must be performed in the daylight hours and can't be over an hour-and-a-half in length.

COLT, HAT/BAT, & OFF-BROADWAY (Chicago Off-Loop Theatre, Hollywood Area Theatre/Bay Area Theatre, and Off-Broadway Theatres, respectively) are the contracts used for the small geographical areas they include. They generally have low wage minimums for the actors because the houses are usually small. Sometimes, however, actors can end up making more money under these contracts than they would under other Equity contracts because the actors not only receive a base salary, but also can receive a bonus which is directly connected to the gross at the box office.

ADTI (American Dinner Theatre Institute, located in Sarasota, Florida) is the negotiating body for Equity Dinner Theatres all over the country. ADTI is also a clearinghouse for these theatres, providing them with information about plays which are being released for possible dinner-theatre consideration, as well as other information of interest to dinner theatres. (There are also non-Equity dinner theatres all over the country which are not affiliated with ADTI. These theatres provide excellent acting experience for the beginning non-Equity actor. An actor can simply call any dinner theatre near him to inquire about auditions. Many times the auditions for these non-Equity theatres are printed in the regular newspapers in the city which houses the theatre.)

When you're reading casting information about the above types of theatres, the contracts used will be referred to as PRODUCTION CONTRACT, LORT, TYA, COLT, HAT/BAT, OFF-BROAD-

WAY, and the DINNER THEATRE CONTRACT, respectively.

All of the Equity theatres are required to have a certain number of EQUITY PRINCIPAL INTERVIEWS which are open to all Equity members (if time allows, they may see non-Equity members as well). Usually these interviews are held two or three times a year, but the number varies from one Equity contract to another. These interviews are not auditions as such. In the screen world, an "interview," by industry jargon, means being seen for a part, where you may or may not actually read. In the stage world, the interview is solely a get-acquainted session where the actor brings his picture and resume, and meets representatives (i.e. casting director, director, producer, etc.) from the production company. These are "general" interviews which may mean the company isn't seeing people for specific roles. In other words, to fulfill a theatre's obligation for the Equity Principal Interview, a theatre producer from Miami might travel to New York twice a year to interview actors for his entire production schedule for that year.

Frankly, few of the roles are actually cast from these principal interviews. Many of the production companies consider the Equity Principal Interview a formality and many of the roles are cast through agents, though of course there are exceptions. The advantage of being seen at the Equity Principal Interview is that you might be kept in mind for future projects. With the smaller companies the interviews take on more importance. To give Equity credit, however, the *main* advantage of the interviews is that you *can get seen* if you're an Equity member, whereas being a member of SAG or AFTRA in no way guarantees you any screen interviews. The basic elimination process for casting (call-backs, etc.) is handled somewhat the same for theatre as for TV and film roles. Usually, however, you don't have to "go through" as many people to get cast in a theatre role as opposed to a screen role; networks, sponsors, etc. But this is *not* to say that it is easier to get cast in a theatre role than in a screen role.

Most of the Equity Principal Interviews are held in New York and/or Los Angeles, even if the theatre is in another city (exception:

BAT and COLT auditions usually are held in San Francisco and Chicago, respectively). That's because so much of the Equity membership is located in these two cities and theatre producers can interview/audition from a large pool of talent there; they have more to choose from. (Also, the theatre producers are required to hold the interviews in a city which has an Equity office.)

Do understand that it is rare for an Equity theatre to cast local talent for major roles. But if there are Equity theatres near you and you want to get into professional theatre, I highly recommend that you try to get into their auditions. There's always a chance that they might see someone they really like, and they might keep that person in mind for the future. The point is, let these theatres know who you are.

Sometimes the Equity theatres will cast a very minor role locally, because it makes good publicity to have a hometown local star working with the professionals. Under the various Equity contracts, Equity theatres are permitted to hire a non-professional or two to act in their productions. The number of non-professionals they can hire is based on a ratio: for example, if there were ten roles to be cast, then under some Equity contracts, the producers could hire one non-professional. (See the Membership Candidate Program in the Eligibility Requirements for Joining AEA, in Appendix C.) Even though these non-professionals are sometimes cast during the principal auditions in New York and/or Los Angeles, at other times a local actor may be able to "break in."

Food For Thought

Whichever medium you pursue, you'll go on many interviews and auditions from which you don't get cast. After every "no" to your face, you'll begin to wonder if you "have it or not," whatever that means. The "no" generally has nothing to do with whether you "have it or not." It simply means you weren't right for that particular part and that particular part only. (Whether this is the actual case or not, which it usually is, actors have to believe this or they run the risk of catching an acute case of "actor's syndrome," or falling prey to the Beverly Theory.)

For instance, let's suppose you go into an audition or interview and you have fair skin and blonde hair. Suppose the producers have already picked the two stars to play the parents in this film and they both have black hair and olive-colored skin. So you read for the part of their son. Chances are you won't get the part because of the "matching" problem. You might have knocked them dead with your reading, but it really won't matter for *that role.* There might be another role in the film you're right for, however, so you always want to give the best interview that you possibly can. BUT, as pointed out in Chapter 1, if you give a bad interview it won't be the end of your career, by any means. You'll be too tall for some parts, too short for others, too big for some parts, and too small for others, and so on. ("Matching" is more of a problem in screen acting than stage acting, but it exists in all of the acting mediums.)

Unfortunately, actors go home from interviews and auditions thinking if they had just read this line a little better, or had just put in this extra facial expression, they might have received the part. But the actor who did get the role might not necessarily have given the best reading. He probably got the part for a number of reasons—he matched physically, he read well, and his personality was probably liked by all.

Your confidence may start to shatter after being too tall, too short, too this, and too that. You'll begin to wonder what's wrong with you. DON'T. You can't take this as a personal attack on your acting.

You'll eventually be "in the right place at the right time,"— meaning in this context, the casting of a show for which the decision makers think you're perfect for the role.

Sometimes you'll hear about a part you're perfect for, but you won't be able to get in on that particular interview or audition. Even if you have a top notch agent, that doesn't necessarily mean you'll get in on that interview. This, too, can be very frustrating. No actor will argue with you on that. But just realize that frustration is a part of an actor's life. When people complain to me about the rough time they're having, I tell them of a theory of which I'm fond. I call it the "Walter Cronkite Theory"—"And that's the way it is." Accept it, and get on with business.

While you're making "the rounds" and interviewing at the studios, you might want to eat! If this is the case, you might want to try acting in COMMERCIALS. Commercial acting is discussed in the next chapter, and it's where the bucks in the acting profession are to be made.

Chapter 7

GETTING INTO COMMERCIALS

I'll never forget that August morning. My agent called and said, "Well, you got the commercial!" I was so beside myself that I didn't even think about the want ads all day.

I phoned the girl I was dating at the time. She wasn't in the acting profession and knew nothing about what I was trying to do. All she knew was that I didn't have a job, and she wondered how I could afford to pay my bills.

"Trish, I got a job!" I yelled through the phone.

"Oh wow, that's terrific. I'm so glad you're working. Who are you working for?"

"I'm working for the Ford Motor Company."

"I didn't know you were mechanically inclined," she muttered.

"No, Trish. You don't understand. I'm going to be in a commercial for Ford."

A long pause, after which she said, "Oh, just a commercial . . . You mean you'll be unemployed again after one day's work?"

Well, she was right. But she, like most people, didn't realize what one day's work on a commercial can do for you financially—or that it comes under the category of ACTING. It's amazing to me how the public perceives the actors who are in commercials. I hear newcomers in the acting business talk about doing some commercials to "tide them over until they can do some real acting." YOU ARE ACTING WHEN YOU'RE IN A COMMERCIAL. You have to create a situation and a likeable character, all in about twenty to thirty seconds' time. This isn't easy!

Check with other actors to get recommendations about commercial workshops in the city in which you plan to act in commercials, if possible. There are a lot of these workshops in the major cities; some of them are terrific and some of them aren't.

In many small and medium-sized cities, you might not find such workshops. But then, sometimes in those cities, you might find it easier to get commercial jobs without special training too. For these jobs you may be working non-union, which means that the information in this chapter about pay-scales, union eligibility, etc., will not apply. Still, you would probably be paid *something,* you'd gain valuable experience, and you'd have tapes to show to prospective agents for the "big time."

Let me point out, however, that commercial tapes aren't generally what TV and film agents want to view from prospective clients, because commercials are very short and really don't show whether the actor can "sustain" a scene or not. Commercial agents, on the other hand, *would* have interest in your commercial tapes.

When you decide you want to go for the "big time," you'll probably find it's easier for the newcomer to get into commercials than into TV entertainment programming or into film. For commercial acting jobs, more actors are interviewed than for film and TV jobs, but remember that the more people allowed into an interview, the better your chances are for getting a foot into the door. Furthermore, commercial producers aren't as fussy about credits as are producers from any other medium. After all, on a commercial interview the interviewer will see your entire thirty-second performance. Also, commercial producers usually care more about getting the right "type" for the part than they do about past experience. Perhaps the main reason commercial producers generally aren't as concerned about past experience as are TV and film producers, is because the commercial will be shot over and over again to get it just the way the advertising agency wants it. Commercial producers sometimes spend a few days on a thirty-second spot. In TV and film acting, however, the scene will only be shot a few times and the actor won't have nearly as many chances.

If you do get cast in a commercial, local or otherwise, have it put on ¾" videotape, the same as with any film that you get on yourself. If you live in a small town which doesn't have franchised agents, you can find out about local commercials from TV stations themselves and from advertising agencies. (Note: Many regional commercials, and *some* local ones, are shot in Los Angeles and New York.)

$ $ $

That one day's work on the commercial can be quite lucrative. People don't realize that more money is made in commercial acting than in TV and film acting. In 1981, $208,257,997 was made in commercials by SAG members; SAG TV actors made $156,933,876, and film actors made $64,375,614. Many actors are paid high into six figures for their ads, and even completely unknown actors can sometimes make into five figures.

An important difference between having a "guest shot" (someone who isn't on a particular show regularly) on entertainment programming, and having a commercial airing, is that the TV show will usually air a few times a year, whereas the commercial may air many times a day. The payments for re-airings of a TV show or commercial are called "residuals."

For acting in a SAG or AFTRA commercial, if you're a principal player and are on-camera, you'll make a minimum of $300 for each day's work. Payment for the first airing of a "Class-A" spot (airs in over twenty cities, and sponsors a TV program) is included as part of the fee you received up-front for the shooting. For that same "Class-A" spot, minimum payments for residuals are the following:

2nd airing: $115.95
3rd-13th airing: $ 92.00
14th and thereafter: $ 44.10

There are many classifications for commercials. You'll be paid each time the commercial airs, unless it's a "wild spot" (meaning it is syndicated and sold separately to each market—non-network). In the case of a "wild spot" commercial, you would be paid a flat sum, in thirteen-week cycles, no matter how many times it airs in those thirteen weeks; the amount depends on how many cities it airs in, the population of those areas, etc. (Note: The majority of commercials are "wild spots.")

Before you decide you want to make a commercial or two a year and think you'll have plenty of money to live on, keep reading, because the plot thickens. It is true that if you could make a few "Class-A" commercials a year *that end up on the air,* you could probably make a decent living.

Just because you shoot a commercial doesn't necessarily mean you will see it on the air. Before hundreds of thousands of dollars are spent putting it on the air, the commercial will be "test-marketed" before audiences to see how effective it is. If you shoot a commercial that doesn't end up on the air, you would still be paid for the day's work. Obviously, though, the real money is to be made in the residuals.

Getting Into Interviews

You must have an agent to get into commercial interviews. There are so many commercial interviews all over New York and Los Angeles, that the actor just isn't able to keep up with what is being cast and where. Again, even if you could keep up with it all, you still wouldn't be able to get yourself into the interviews anyway. (Basically, my discussion here is for commercials cast in New York and Los Angeles, which are the major commercial markets.

However, many commercials are cast in other cities as well. In cities that have franchised agents, actors should *still* try to get hooked up with an agent. Most advertising agencies would rather deal with agents.)

Most commercial casting calls do not appear on the Breakdown Services. In Los Angeles, there is a computerized service called "Commercial Breakthrough/In-Touch," which sends messages each day to teleprinters in commercial agents' offices. This service, like the Breakdown Services, gives the vital information about the casting to agents. Many commercial casting directors in New York and Los Angeles simply call a few of their favorite commercial agents directly to let them know what types they need for a particular commercial. This is why you'll get few, if any, commercial interviews in New York or Los Angeles without an agent. Also, rarely can an actor get a general interview with a commercial casting director in Los Angeles. Most advertising agencies in LA usually hire an independent casting director for each commercial, and since the casting directors are running from one ad to the next, they rarely have time to chat with actors. In New York, however, many advertising agencies have casting directors on staff, and therefore are more likely to have some general interviews, though usually an agent needs to set them up.

Before searching for a commercial agent, know what "type" you are. Whether you're big, small, bald, hairy, fat, or skinny; whether you can model designers' clothes or duffle bags; there is still a place for you in the commercial field. Commercials use every conceivable type. BE WHAT YOU ARE!

Once you've decided what type you are and you have a head shot to represent that type, start sending the head shot out to commercial agents. You'll also want to attach a resume to the picture even though after you get a commercial agent, the resume will rarely be used.

A composite would give the agent a better idea of your type than a head shot only, but as pointed out earlier, the agent will probably want changes in it, anyway. So you'll be saving yourself a lot of money by holding off on the composite until you get a commercial agent, who will help you put it together. After all, that agent has to sell you and he knows what casting directors are looking for in your photos.

Once you have a commercial agent, you should be sure to re-do your commercial resume to exclude commercial credits. (Keep in mind that your agent will rarely use the resume, but most of them want a few, just in case a commercial producer wants to see your acting credits.) When you re-do your commercial resume, simply state "Commercials: List Upon Request," as discussed in Chapter 3. You don't want to take a chance of losing out on a job because of the casting director thinking you have a "product conflict."

For instance, if you list a Coke commercial on your resume and you are being considered for a 7-Up commercial, you might have a conflict of interest. If you have a Coke commercial running on the air, YOU CAN'T BE IN ANY COMMERCIAL THAT CON-FLICTS WITH THAT PRODUCT, until you have been released from the Coke commercial. DON'T EVEN TRY! If you list the Coke commercial on your commercial resume, the ad agency might think you haven't been released from the Coke ad when in fact you might have been.

If you have an ad that isn't airing, but you're still being "held" for it, you'll still be paid. This money is called a "holding fee." You are being paid this compensation for the fact that you can't work for any competing product and you're not making any residual money on the ad since it isn't airing yet. For every thirteen weeks you're being held, you'll be paid the holding fee which is equal to your session fee for that commercial (i.e. one day's pay). An ad agency can hold you for 21 months. If the ad agency wants to keep holding you after that time, it has to renegotiate with you.

During the Interview

Your commercial agent will phone you when he has an interview set up for you with an advertising agency. Generally the agent will give you a few sentences' description of the character for which you'll be interviewing. You want to dress somewhat like the character would dress. You want to give the ad agency and the casting director the idea that you are the character they want.

Arrive for the interview early. As with most TV and film interviews, scripts for commercials aren't sent out to the actors in advance (unless you're a star and your services are requested for the ad). If you get to the interview early, chances are you'll have more time to look over the script.

When you first walk into a commercial interview, you'll sign in on the "sign-in" sheet. You'll list your name, agent, social security number, and time in. For SAG and AFTRA commercials, if the advertising agency or casting director keeps you for over an hour, you'll be paid $18.75 in half-hour increments. (There is no payment for the first hour, whether it be the initial interview or the first callback.) In other words, if you're on the interview for an hour and three minutes, you'll be paid $18.75. If you're on the interview for an hour and thirty-five minutes, you'll be paid $37.50, and so on. SAG and AFTRA will have a record of how long you were on the interview because the "sign-in" sheets will be sent to them; your payment if you're kept overtime will come by check weeks later. (All of the above figures are standard rates set by SAG and AFTRA and are NOT negotiable. The rates apply to any SAG and AFTRA commercial be it local, syndicated, cable, or network.)

If the commercial is being filmed in a small city, it might be a non-union commercial. This being the case, you'll probably receive a flat fee for the commercial with no residuals and no payments for overtime at the auditions. (Note: If you're a member of SAG then you can't be in a non-SAG commercial that is shot on film, and if you're a member of AFTRA, you can't be in a non-AFTRA commercial that is shot on tape.)

When you walk into the actual interview, after signing your name and other vital statistics, you'll give your composite to the casting director and/or producer, director, etc. They will probably just talk to you for a few minutes. They want to learn something about your personality; they want to determine whether you are likeable before they cast you in their commercial. They realize that if the public doesn't like the people in the commercial, the commercial won't be very successful.

As in all commercials, the actor should be very "up." It is most important that on a commercial interview the actor has a lot of energy. A sense of humor is always a plus, too. Being laid back on a commercial interview is usually a killer. Be bright and happy. Be friendly and act as if you are having a terrific time, even though you may hate the product you are trying to sell. I can think of so many commercial interviews where I looked at the awful food I was trying to sell and couldn't decide if I should eat it, or set it free. However, you must act as though the product is truly wonderful.

You will be on tape for only a few minutes at most. First you'll "slate your name and agent." This simply means that when the camera rolls, you state your name and that of your agent. Then you might just swing your head from the left to the right and back. Or you might deliver the entire commercial on-camera. Sometimes the interviewers will ask you to "improv" a commercial for their product; meaning that you act out the commercial on-the-spot using your own thoughts and dialogue. If you do an improv, the idea is to be different. DON'T BE BORING. Again, humor is always welcomed. (If you are requested to improvise dialogue, legally you should be notified in advance and should be paid a small fee. Ask your agent for details.)

Sometimes you'll be by yourself on camera and other times you'll be with other actors. Many times the casting director will take in five or six actors at a time, who are all up for the same part, and put them all on camera at once. The reason for this is so the people from the ad agency can see the different "types" together and get an idea who stands out. You want to stand out from the rest of the crowd and make a quick impression. Smile, and think warm thoughts. Think to yourself, "I'd really like to work with you. I really like your product." If you keep these warm thoughts in your mind, usually your face will come to light!

During the interview you may be asked if you have a certain skill. For instance, they might need a sky diver in a particular commercial. IF YOU CAN'T SKY DIVE, THEN DON'T SAY YOU CAN. Everyone involved with the commercial will eventually find out anyway.

That kind of problem came up when I was interviewing for a Honda commercial and was asked if I could drive a motorcycle. I not only don't know how to drive a motorcycle, but I'm scared to death of them. In my eagerness for the job, however, I said yes, I could drive one. I WAS CAST IN THE COMMERCIAL! When we started shooting the actual commercial, I ran over the director's foot. The director just didn't have much of a sense of humor limping around on one foot all day, and after the shooting he swung by St. Joseph's Hospital for a check-up. As you can well imagine, I haven't worked for that director since . . .

You'll leave the interview and sign out on the "sign-in" sheet. Generally, you'll hear from the ad agency, through your agent, within a day or so if you are wanted on a call-back. (In some cases, the interview tape is sent to the ad agency, which may be housed in a different city. In these cases, it could take longer to hear from them.)

Call-Backs

On the call-back DON'T DRASTICALLY CHANGE YOUR APPEARANCE. Basically you should dress and act the same way you did on the original interview. Obviously you are close to what the casting director and/or ad agency people want if they're calling you back. There's really no way to prepare for the call-back, unless you "accidentally" walk off with the script they gave you on the original interview. Usually the script is so short, however, that you'll have it memorized before you leave the first interview. The call-back is usually very similar to the original interview, but fewer people are now in competition for the part. Again, if you're on a union commercial interview for over an hour you'll be paid $18.75 in half-hour increments.

If you are called back a third time (second call-back), you'll be paid $75.00 for just showing up and if the agency keeps you for over two hours, you'll be paid $18.75 for each half-hour over the two. And if you're called back a fourth time (third call-back), you'll be paid $150.00 for any time under four hours. (All of the above figures are standard rates and aren't negotiable.) Ad agencies will rarely have two call-backs and will rarely keep you for over an hour. Usually commercials are cast from the first call-back (second interview), sometimes even from the first interview.

Unions and Commercials

If you're cast in a commercial as a "principal player," and the commercial is shot on film (as most of them are), you are eligible to join SAG. In commercial work, if the actor is on-camera and is identified with the product, demonstrates the product, or reacts to the message in the commercial, he might be considered a principal player without mouthing a word. If an actor is considered an extra by the ad agency, but the actor himself thinks he's a principal by the above definition, he can file a claim with SAG; the claims department will view the commercial in question and make that decision. (If you're cast as an extra in a commercial in a city where SEG has jurisdiction you still must follow the procedure for joining SEG as outlined earlier.)

If the commercial is shot on tape, whether a principal or an extra, you're working under the jurisdiction of AFTRA. If you're a principal in an AFTRA commercial (the distinction between extra and principal and the right to file a claim are the same as above), you're eligible to join SAG because you've had a principal role under AFTRA's jurisdiction as opposed to just running down to one of AFTRA's offices and handing them the bucks. However, as stated earlier, you must wait one year from the time you had the AFTRA job, before you can join SAG.

Voice-Overs

Another way to go in commercials is "voice-overs." Voice-over actors are actors who talk, but who aren't seen, though many actors who do voice-over work also do on-camera acting. Next time you're in front of the tube, watch some commercials and you'll hear announcers whom you don't see.

One advantage of voice-over work is that you can *sometimes* have product conflicts that are legal. You usually aren't as associated with the product in a voice-over as you are when you're in front of the camera. BUT, the general rule of thumb is that the voices between two competing products must not be identifiable with each other. In other words, if you did a character voice in one ad, and a straight voice in the competing ad, this might be perfectly legal. However, you must clear this product conflict with the companies you're working for.

There's a lot of work for voice-over actors—commercials, cartoons, TV narration, and radio, to name some possibilities. Voice-over work calls for a very specialized talent, and you really have to be able to use your voice well to get cast in this field. Generally, it's not a field that the beginner can "jump right into," but rather a field where proven professionals are used.

Many of the principles used in getting work as a visible actor generally apply to obtaining work as a voice-over actor (radio and otherwise). For instance, one still must obtain an agent, and the differences between obtaining an agent for the other acting fields as opposed to the voice-over areas are outlined below.

Most voice-over agents are associated with commercial agents. In other words, some big commercial agencies have a separate department specifically for voice-over work. Simply check with commercial agents and ask if they have a voice-over department. To seek representation, send agents your resume and a tape of your voice. DO NOT MAKE A TAPE THAT SOUNDS HOME-MADE! If you do the recording yourself, make sure it sounds professional. An amateur-sounding recording is to the voice-over industry what a bad photograph is to the theatrical industry: it does more harm than good. Do readings of material that suit your voice best—commercial readings, animated voices, etc. The tape should be REEL-TO-REEL and shouldn't be over five minutes in length.

This tape is your passport to the voice-over industry as photographs are to the acting industry. Once you have an agent, he'll be submitting this tape to voicecasters (casting directors for voice-over work) for potential jobs. Many times the voicecaster will send the material he wants read to your agent. Your agent will have a few actors in to record the material for the voicecaster; most voice-over agents have reel-to-reel machines in their offices and recordings for a specific job can be recorded right there. Other times you might go to the voicecaster's or the ad agency's office to audition.

* * * * * * *

For many actors, commercials are the end. Some actors only want to be in commercials, and some of them are extremely successful at it. But for other actors, commercials are a way to make money while waiting for that "big break."

Publisher's Note: For a comprehensive treatment of commercial acting, read Tom Logan's second book, ACTING IN THE MILLION DOLLAR MINUTE. The Art & Business of Performing in TV Commercials. *That book deals with matters such as script terms and how a commercial is shot, guidance on dialogue delivery and physical staging, handling the product, and other aspects of the Art. It also covers Business matters such as agents, contracts, and unions; the commercial interview process from the moment you walk in the door through your thank-you notes after you leave; and the working conditions you can expect.*

THAT'S A WRAP

Let me say that I wish you all the luck in the world. The mere fact that you took the time to read this book is evidence that you at least have some determination. By now you know what to look out for in this business. I hope I have been of some help to you—you have been to me; you bought my book. But I know it will save you a lot of time, trouble, and money.

By all means I don't mean to play down the talent end of the acting business. Talent is very important, but talent alone will do you little good, if any, without a winning personality and a good business knowledge of how the entertainment industry works.

As time moves on and you're looking for acting jobs, don't become a victim of the Beverly Theory. You aren't alone if you're having a hard time finding work as an actor. All you have to do is look around you and you'll see many actors unemployed. And consider the following statistics from the Screen Actors Guild, for 1981. These earnings figures are the most recent available, and the percentages are indicative of SAG employment every year. (Such statistics are not available from AFTRA or Equity.)

57.9% of the members earned less than $1,000 annually
81.7% earned less than $5,000 annually

88.5% earned less than $10,000 annually
2.4% earned more than $50,000 annually

The above figures don't include *all* the actors who are trying to get work. They include only professional actors who are already members of the Screen Actors Guild. If you add all the actors who are trying to get into the business, the statistics would even be worse.

It's just a fact that, to keep food on the table, most actors have to have other jobs, working as doctors, cab drivers, bartenders, insurance and real estate salesmen, undertakers, waiters/waitresses, etc. Unfortunately, they often have a hard time holding down jobs because they're running around on interviews and auditions. Employers don't think too highly of this.

Whenever you do work, however, you'll be paid well. The pay scales vary, but for stage work, under Equity contracts, you'll be making minimums from $150 to $725 per week, depending on the Equity contract used. As a principal player in TV and film, you'll make at least a few hundred dollars—PER DAY. As we discussed, every time your Class-A network commercial airs on TV, you can probably at least pay that month's phone bill. You might wonder, then, how come the statistics show that actors make so little money. The problem is that work is extremely hard to find and most actors only work a few days a year as evidenced by the grueling statistics. So when you're "pounding the pavement" for work, just realize that you are not alone.

Whatever you do—RELAX. Getting all depressed and bent out of shape will only defeat your purposes. If a certain agent doesn't take you on as a client, you'll find another agent. If a producer doesn't want you for a certain part, you'll find another part. Granted, it is sometimes hard to keep a positive attitude under such circumstances, but you *must* learn to cope with rejection. There have been so many times I've been upset because I didn't get a certain part I really wanted. What a waste of precious time! It makes no difference now, and to tell you the truth, I can't even single out *one* of those times.

Accept the reality of show business, but be optimistic and know you have something to offer to the public. Facing reality with a positive attitude is better than living in a fantasy that someone will "discover" you. "Discover" yourself. I hear people say it takes luck to make it in this business. They may be right. And you may get that lucky break—but if you are not prepared for it, what good would it do?

You may never be a household name, but if you follow the principles I've set forth in this book, chances are that you'll eventually get work as a professional actor. Forget that you want to be a "star." If that is meant to happen to you, then in due time it will. Otherwise, feel proud that you will accomplish what many people only dream of—to work in the greatest profession in the world, ACTING.

SEE YA ON THE SET.

APPENDICES

Appendix A

OFFICES OF SAG, AFTRA, AND EQUITY

Locations of offices are presented in alphabetical order, first by state, and then, within each state, by city. To find the specific geographical area covered by a particular office, contact the office directly.

ACTORS' EQUITY ASSOCIATION (EQUITY, OR AEA)

National Office
165 W. 46th St.
New York, NY 10036
(212) 869-8530

Western
6430 Sunset Blvd., #616
Hollywood, CA 90028
(213) 462-2334

182 2nd St.
San Francisco, CA 94105
(415) 974-5594

Midwest
360 N. Michigan Ave., #1401
Chicago, IL 60601
(312) 641-0393

AMERICAN FEDERATION OF TELEVISION
AND RADIO ARTISTS

National Office
Sanford I. Wolff, Esq., National Exec. Sec.
1350 Avenue of the Americas
New York, NY 10019
(212) 265-7700

Locals and Chapters

Arizona
Mr. Donald Livesay, Exec. Sec.
3030 N. Central, #301
Phoenix, AZ 85012
(602) 279-9975

California
Kenneth Clarke, Pres.
4418 E. Austin Way
Fresno, CA 93726
(209) 224-8929

Mr. Allan H. Davis, Exec. Sec.
1717 N. Highland Ave.
Hollywood, CA 90028
(213) 461-8111

Ms. Jacqueline Walters, Exec. Sec.
3045 Rosecrans St., #308
San Diego, CA 92110
(714) 222-1161

c/o KOVR-TV
1216 Arden Way
Sacramento, CA 95815
(916) 927-1313

Donald S. Tayer, Esq., Exec. Sec.
and Counsel
100 Bush St.
San Francisco, CA 94104
(415) 391-7510

Colorado
Jerre Hookey, Exec. Sec.
6825 E. Tennessee, #639
Denver, CO 80224
(303) 388-4287

Connecticut
Mr. Peter Halladay, Steward
c/o Station WSTC
117 Prospect St.
Stamford, CT 06901
(203) 327-1400

District of Columbia
Ms. Evelyn Freyman, Exec. Sec.
35 Wisconsin Circle, #210
Washington, DC 20015
(301) 657-2560

Florida
Ms. Diane Hogan, Asst. Exec. Sec.
70 N.E. 167th St.
North Miami Beach, FL 33162
(305) 940-8543; (305) 940-8578;
(305) 940-8606

Georgia
Mr. Thomas Even, Exec. Sec.
3110 Maple Dr. N.E., #210
Atlanta, GA 30305
(404) 237-0831; (404) 237-9961

Hawaii
Ms. Brenda Chayra
P.O. Box 1350
Honolulu, HI 96807
(808) 533-2652

Illinois
Mr. Herb Neuer, Exec. Sec.
307 N. Michigan Ave.
Chicago, IL 60601
(312) 372-8081

AFTRA Offices (continued)

Mr. Kenneth Killebrew, Pres.
Station WEEK
2907 Springfield Rd.
East Peoria, IL 61611
(309) 699-5052

Indiana

Mr. Irving Fink, Exec. Sec.
Dutton, Kappes, & Overman
20 N. Meridian St., 7th Floor
Indianapolis, IN 46204
(317) 635-5395

826 S. 25th St.
South Bend, IN 46615
(219) 232-9553

Kentucky

Mr. John V. Hanley, Exec. Sec.
730 W. Main St., #250
Louisville, KY 40202
(502) 584-6594

Louisiana

Ms. Pauline Morgan, Exec. Sec.
1108 Royal St.
New Orleans, LA 70116
(504) 524-9903

Maryland

Bernard Rubenstein, Esq.
10 Light St., #1145
Baltimore, MD 21202
(301) 752-6160

Massachusetts

Mr. Robert Segal, Exec. Sec.
11 Beacon St., #1000
Boston, MA 02108
(617) 742-0208; (617) 742-2688

Michigan

Ms. Mary Ann Formaz, Exec. Sec.
24901 N. Western Hwy.
Heritage Plaza Office Bldg., #406
Southfield, MI 48075
(313) 354-1774

Minnesota

Mr. John Kailin, Exec. Sec.
2500 Park Avenue South, Ste. A
Minneapolis, MN 55404
(612) 871-2404

Missouri

Ms. Caroline Noble, Exec. Sec.
406 W. 34th St., #310
Kansas City, MO 64111
(816) 753-4557

Mr. Larry Ward, Exec. Sec.
Paul Brown Bldg.
818 Olive St., #1237
St. Louis, MO 63101
(314) 231-8410

New York

Mr. Alex Roberts, Pres.
Oxford Heights #9
Albany, NY 12203
(518) 385-1284; (518) 385-1385

Mr. Jim Gagliardi, Steward
c/o Station WROW-AM
341 Northern Blvd.
Albany, NY 12204
(518) 436-4841

Mr. Doug Meyers
c/o Station WTEN-TV
P.O. Box 10
Albany, NY 12201
(518) 436-4822

Mr. Bob Buchanan, Steward
c/o Station WBNG-TV
50 Front St.
Binghamton, NY 13905
(607) 723-7311

Mr. Stanford M. Silverberg, Exec. Sec.
Silverberg, Silverberg, Yood,
& Sellers
635 Brisbane Bldg.
Buffalo, NY 14203
(716) 854-6495

AFTRA Offices (continued)

Ms. Marie Rice, Pres.
WIVB-TV
2077 Elmwood Ave.
Buffalo, NY 14207
(716) 874-4410

Ms. Marsha Boyd, Exec. Sec.
One Exchange St., #900
Rochester, NY 14614
(716) 325-3175

Mr. Earl Pudney, Sec., Treas.
c/o Station WGY-WRGB
1400 Balltown Rd.
Schenectady, NY 12309
(518) 385-1284

Ohio
Ms. Fernanda Crudo, Exec. Sec.
1814-16 Carew Tower
Cincinnati, OH 45202
(513) 579-8668

Mr. Kenneth Bichl, Exec. Sec.
1367 E. 6th St.
#229, The Lincoln Bldg.
Cleveland, OH 44114
(216) 781-2255

Oregon
Ms. Artha Adair, Exec. Sec.
915 N.E. Davis St.
Portland, OR 97232
(503) 238-6914

Pennsylvania
Mr. Glenn A. Goldstein, Exec. Sec.
1405 Locust St., #811
Philadelphia, PA 19102
(215) 732-0507

Mr. Dan Mallinger, Exec. Sec.
62 Stanwix St.
Pittsburgh, PA 15222
(412) 281-6767

Tennessee
Mr. David Maddox, Exec. Sec.
P.O. Box 121087, Acklen Station
United Artists Tower, #404
50 Music Square West
Nashville, TN 37212
(615) 327-2947

Texas
Ms. Clinta Dayton, Exec. Sec.
3220 Lemmon Ave., #102
Dallas, TX 75204
(214) 522-2080; (214) 522-2085

Ms. Claire Gordon, Exec. Sec.
2620 Fountainview, #214
Houston, TX 77057
(713) 972-1806

Washington
Ms. Carol Matt, Exec. Sec.
P.O. Box 9688
158 Thomas St.
Seattle, WA 98109
(206) 624-7340

Wisconsin
Ms. Irene Nelson
929 52nd St.
Kenosha, WI 53140

SCREEN ACTORS GUILD

National Office
7750 Sunset Blvd.
Hollywood, CA 90046
(213) 876-3030

SAG Offices (continued)

Arizona
3030 N. Central, #919
Phoenix, AZ 85012
(602) 279-9975

California
3045 Rosecrans, #308
San Diego, CA 92110
(714) 222-3996

100 Bush St., 26th Floor
San Francisco, CA 94104
(415) 391-7510

Colorado
6825 E. Tennessee Ave., #639
Denver, CO 80222
(303) 388-4287

Florida
145 Madeira Ave., #317
Coral Gables, FL 33134
(305) 444-7677

Georgia
3110 Maple Dr., N.E., #210
Atlanta, GA 30305
(404) 237-9961

Illinois
307 N. Michigan Ave.
Chicago, IL 60601
(312) 372-8081

Maryland (serves D.C.)
35 Wisconsin Circle, #210
Chevy Chase, MD 20015
(301) 657-2560

Massachusetts
11 Beacon St., #1000
Boston, MA 02108
(617) 742-2688

Michigan
28690 Southfield Rd.
Lathrup Village, MI 48076
(313) 559-9540

Minnesota
2500 Park Ave., Ste. A*
Minneapolis, MN 55402
(612) 871-2404

Missouri
406 W. 34th St., #310*
Kansas City, MO 64111
(816) 753-4557

818 Olive St., #617*
St. Louis, MO 63101
(314) 231-8410

New York
1700 Broadway, 18th Floor
New York, NY 10019
(212) 957-5370

Ohio
1367 E. 6th St.*
Cleveland, OH 44114
(216) 781-2255

Pennsylvania
1405 Locust St., #811
Philadelphia, PA 19102
(215) 545-3150

Tennessee
P.O. Box 121087
Nashville, TN 37212
(615) 327-2944

Texas
3220 Lemmon Ave., #102
Dallas, TX 75204
(214) 522-2080

2620 Fountainview, #215
Houston, TX 77057
(713) 972-1806

Washington
158 Thomas St.*
Seattle, WA 98109
(206) 624-7340

*AFTRA offices which handle SAG for their area.

Appendix B

ELIGIBILITY REQUIREMENTS FOR SAG

7750 Sunset Blvd.
Hollywood, CA 90046
(213) 876-3030

An actor may become eligible for Screen Actors Guild membership under one of the following conditions:

1. If the applicant is NOT a member of an affiliated Guild, he or she must present a letter from a SAG signatory motion picture producer or his representative, or from a film television or commercial company, stating that the applicant is wanted for a principal role or speaking part in a specific film, not more than two weeks prior to the beginning of filming.

    The joining fee is $637.50 of which $600.00 represents the initiation fee and $37.50 is for the current semi-annual dues period.

2. If the applicant is a currently paid-up member in good standing of an affiliated Guild (Equity, AFTRA, AGMA, AGVA, SEG, etc.) for a period of at least one year or longer and has worked as a principal performer in that jurisdiction at least once, OR:

    If the applicant has not been a member of an affiliated Guild for a minimum period of one year, BUT has a definite commitment for a principal role or speaking part in a motion picture, filmed commercial, or filmed television show, he or she will be accepted for membership into the Screen Actors Guild, not more than two weeks prior to the beginning of filming of his or her part.

The joining fee is determined at the time of application to Screen Actors Guild and may be based on the amount of initiation fee paid to the affiliated Guild.

3. If the applicant has proof or employment by a SAG signatory motion picture production company or film television or commercial company in a principal role or speaking part which states the applicant's name and social security number, the signatory company's name, the name of the production or the commercial (the product), the salary paid (in dollar-amount form), and the specific date(s) worked, he or she will be accepted for membership. Such proof of employment may be in the form of a signed contract, a payroll check and/or stub, or a letter from the company (on the company's letterhead stationery) provided it states all the necessary information listed in this paragraph. (Original or carbon copies, not photocopies, are accepted.)

The joining fee is determined at the time of application for Screen Actors Guild by the method stated in paragraph 1 or 2 above.

FIRST JOB AS A PRINCIPAL CAN DENOTE WHICH GUILD IS PARENT AND THAT UNION IS TO RECEIVE FULL INITIATION FEES AND DUES.

Please NOTE: All joining fees are payable in full in cash, cashier's check, or money order at the time of application. NO personal checks are accepted for joining fees.

If you are eligible under the conditions stated above and wish to make application for Screen Actors Guild membership, please call our office BEFORE COMING IN so we may advise you of the amount of your joining fee and arrange an appointment for you with our New Membership Department. At the time of your appointment, please allow at least 45 to 60 minutes to complete the application procedures and paperwork.

For current update, check with the Screen Actors Guild.

From the New Membership Department

Printed by special permission from the Screen Actors Guild.

Appendix C

ELIGIBILITY REQUIREMENTS FOR EQUITY

165 W. 46th St.
New York, NY 10036
(212) 869-8530

How do I become an Equity Actor/Actress, Chorus Performer, or Stage Manager?

There are two ways:

1. You are hired to work in an Equity show. The producer, who has agreed to conform to Equity conditions for a production in our jurisdiction, gives you a standard Equity contract, which he or she has signed. You present the contract to Equity, fill out an application, pay your initiation fee and dues, and receive a temporary membership card. Your application is submitted to Council, and when Council has acted upon it favorably, your permanent AEA membership card will be sent to you.

2. You join the Equity Membership Candidate Program at one of the many participating Equity theatres. The Membership Candidate (MC) Program allows non-professional actors and stage managers to credit their work towards AEA membership. After fifty (50) weeks of such work, the registered MC is eligible to join AEA.

    The fifty weeks need not be consecutive and may be

accumulated over any length of time at any number of participating theatres. The program is presently in effect at many Equity Dinner, Resident, and Stock Theatres, where a Membership Candidate may receive credit for weeks spent in rehearsal and performance time as an actor, understudy, or production assistant.

When you have secured a non-professional position at an Equity theatre that participates in the MC program, you register as an MC by completing an Equity non-professional affidavit provided by the theatre, and sending to Equity the affidavit and a $50 registration fee payable to AEA. This one-time fee is credited against the initiation fee that will become due when you are eligible to join AEA. Once you are properly registered as an MC, Equity records all work-weeks as reported by the theatre management.

When you have accumulated fifty work-weeks as an MC, your eligibility to join Equity will last for a five-year period. But you may no longer work at an Equity theatre unless you have signed an Equity contract and joined Equity.

As the Membership Candidate is not yet a member of Equity, but rather, is working towards membership, the protections and privileges enjoyed by AEA members cannot be extended to the MC. Thus, you may not attend Principal Interviews and Auditions with AEA members, and there are no established salaries or benefits for the MC, except those agreed upon between the individual and the theatre management.

Special application must be made in advance to Equity for permission to work as a Membership Candidate if the individual is currently or has been at any time in the past a member of any of the entertainment industry unions under the 4-A's jurisdiction.

What does it cost to become an Equity member?

The initiation fee as of November 1, 1981, of $500 and minimum half-yearly dues of $26 are payable upon joining, by cash, certified check, or money order. Thereafter, dues are payable on May 1st and November 1st and vary according to your income under Equity jurisdiction. If you have worked as a member of one of the other entertainment industry unions prior to joining Equity, you pay reduced fees to AEA.

For further information on fees and joining Equity with a contract, contact the Membership Department. For questions or problems relating to the Membership Candidate Program, write or call the Membership Candidate Department.

From the Department of Membership Education and Communication

Printed by special permission from Actors' Equity Association.

Appendix D

THEATRES WHERE EQUITY'S MEMBERSHIP CANDIDATE PROGRAM MAY BE IN EFFECT

The following Equity theatres may use the Membership Candidate Program. At these theatres, when there exists a ratio of so many non-Equity actors for so many Equity actors, the non-Equity actors may have their work credited towards membership in Actors' Equity Association.

THIS LIST IS NOT COMPLETE AND IS SUBJECT TO CHANGE; PROSPECTIVE MEMBERSHIP CANDIDATES SHOULD INQUIRE AT A THEATRE IN ADVANCE WHETHER OR NOT THE PROGRAM IS IN EFFECT.

In addition to the theatres cited below, Membership Candidates should be aware that the Program may be used at certain Chicago Off-Loop Theatres (COLT), Hollywood Area Theatres (HAT), Bay Area Theatres (BAT), and Resident Indoor Musical Stock Theatres (RIMST).

LEAGUE OF RESIDENT THEATRES (LORT)

Alabama
Alabama Shakespeare Festival
P.O. Box 141
Anniston, AL 36202

Alaska
Alaska Repertory Theatre
523 W. 8th Ave., #110
Anchorage, AK 99501

EMC Theatres (continued)

Arizona
Arizona Theatre Company
120 W. Broadway
Tucson, AZ 85701

California
Berkeley Shakespeare Festival
P.O. Box 5328
Berkeley, CA 94705

South Coast Repertory Theatre
655 S. Town Center Dr.
Costa Mesa, CA 92626

L.A. Public Theatre
P.O. Box 1951
Los Angeles, CA 90028

California Actors' Theatre
P.O. Box 1355
Los Gatos, CA 95030

Old Globe Theatre
P.O. Box 2171
San Diego, CA 92112

California Shakespeare Festival
417 N. Locust St.
Box 590
Visalia, CA 93277

Colorado
Denver Center for Performing Arts
c/o Denver Center Theatre Company
1050 13th St.
Denver, CO 80204

Connecticut
The New Globe Theatre
111 Wheeler Park Ave.
Fairfield, CT 06432

Hartford Stage Company
50 Church St.
Hartford, CT 06103

Long Wharf Theatre
222 Sargent Dr.
New Haven, CT 06511

Yale Repertory Theatre
Yale School of Drama
New Haven, CT 06520

Hartman Theatre Company
Box 521
Stamford, CT 06901

Eugene O'Neill Memorial
     Theatre Center
(Nat'l Playwrights Conference)
P.O. Box 206
Waterford, CT 06385
(summer)

District of Columbia
Arena Stage
6th & M Sts., S.W.
Washington, DC 20024

Folger Theatre Group
201 E. Capitol St., S.E.
Washington, DC 20003

Florida
The Caldwell Theatre Company
P.O. Box 277
Boca Raton, FL 33432

Players State Theatre
Coconut Grove Playhouse
3500 Main Hwy.
Miami, FL 33133

Asolo Theatre Festival
P.O. Drawer E
Sarasota, FL 33578

Georgia
Alliance Theatre Company
1280 Peachtree St., N.E.
Atlanta, GA 30309

Illinois
Goodman Theatre Company
200 S. Columbus Dr.
Chicago, IL 60603

LORT Theatres (continued)

North Light Repertory Company
2300 Green Bay Rd.
Evanston, IL 60201

Illinois Theatre Center
400 Lakewood Blvd.
Park Forest, IL 60466

Indiana
Indiana Repertory Company
140 W. Washington St.
Indianapolis, IN 46204

Kentucky
Horse Cave Theatre
P.O. Box 215
Horse Cave, KY 42749
(summer)

Actors Theatre of Louisville
316-320 W. Main St.
Louisville, KY 40202

Maryland
Center Stage
700 N. Calvert St.
Baltimore, MD 21202

Massachusetts
American Repertory Theatre Company
64 Brattle St.
Cambridge, MA 02138

Shakespeare and Company
The Mount
Plunkett St.
Lenox, MA 01240
(summer)

Merrimack Regional Theatre
P.O. Box 228
Lowell, MA 01853

Stage West
1511 Memorial Ave.
West Springfield, MA 01089

Michigan
Meadow Brook Theatre
Oakland University
Rochester, MI 48063

Minnesota
Cricket Theatre
Hennepin Center for Arts
528 Hennepin Ave.
Minneapolis, MN 55403

Actors Theatre of St. Paul
2115 Summit Ave.
St. Paul, MN 55105

Missouri
Arrow Rock Lyceum Theatre
Arrow Rock, MO 63520
(summer)

Missouri Repertory Theatre
University of Missouri at K.C.
5100 Rockhill Rd.
Kansas City, MO 64110

Loretto-Hilton Theatre
130 Edgar Rd.
St. Louis, MO 63119

Montana
Montana Repertory Theatre
University of Montana
Missoula, MT 59812

New Hampshire
Theatre By The Sea
125 Bow St.
Portsmouth, NH 03801
(LORT rules winter season,
CORST rules summer season)

New Jersey
New Jersey Shakespeare Festival
Drew University
Madison, NJ 07940
(summer and fall)

LORT Theatres (continued)

George St. Playhouse
414 George St.
New Brunswick, NJ 08901

McCarter Theatre Company, Inc.
91 University Pl.
Princeton University
Princeton, NJ 08540

New York
League of Theatre Artists
P.O. Box 2114
Empire State Plaza
Albany, NY 12203

Studio Arena Theatre
710 Main St.
Buffalo, NY 14202

Westchester Regional Theatre
229 Harrison Ave.
Harrison, NY 10528

Center for Music, Drama and Art
Saranac Ave. at Fawn Ridge
Lake Placid, NY 12946

Negro Ensemble Company
165 W. 46th St.
New York, NY 10036

New York Shakespeare Festival
(Delacorte and Mobile Theatre)
The Public Theatre
425 Lafayette St.
New York, NY 10003
(summer)

Playwrights Horizons (Queens)
416 W. 42nd St.
New York, NY 10036

Roundabout Theatre Company
333 W. 23rd St.
New York, NY 10011

Genessee Valley Arts Foundation
(GeVa)
168 Clinton Ave. South
Rochester, NY 14604

Syracuse Stage
University Regent Theatre
820 E. Genessee St.
Syracuse, NY 13210

North Carolina
Playmakers Repertory Company
103 South Bldg.
University of N.C. at Chapel Hill
Chapel Hill, NC 27514

Ohio
Playhouse in the Park
P.O. Box 6537
Cincinnati, OH 45206

Cleveland Playhouse
2040 E. 86th St.
Cleveland, OH 44106

Great Lakes Shakespeare Festival
P.O. Box 598
Edgewater
Cleveland, OH 44107

Kenyon Repertory Theatre
and Festival
302 W. Brooklyn
Gambier, OH 43022

Pennsylvania
Pennsylvania Stage Company
J.I. Rodale Theatre
837 Linden St.
Allentown, PA 18101

Philadelphia Drama Guild
220 S. 16th St.
Philadelphia, PA 19102

Pittsburgh Public Theatre
1 Allegheny Sq., #230
Pittsburgh, PA 15212

Rhode Island
Trinity Square Repertory Company
201 Washington St.
Providence, RI 02903

LORT Theatres (continued)

Tennessee
Clarence Brown Theatre Company
Dept. of Speech and Theatre
206 McClung Tower
University of Tennessee
Knoxville, TN 37916

Texas
Theatre 3
2800 Routh St.
Dallas, TX 75201

Alley Theatre
615 Texas Ave.
Houston, TX 77002

Virginia
Barter Theatre
Abingdon, VA 24210

Wayside Theatre
P.O. Box 260
Middletown, VA 22657

Virginia Stage Company
142 W. York St.
Norfolk, VA 23510

Virginia Museum Theatre
Boulevard & Grove Aves.
Richmond, VA 23221

Washington
A Contemporary Theatre
709 1st Ave. West
Seattle, WA 98119

Intiman Theatre
Box 4246
Seattle, WA 98119

Seattle Repertory Theatre
P.O. Box B
Queen Anne Station
Seattle Center
Seattle, WA 98109

Wisconsin
Milwaukee Repertory Theatre
Performing Arts Center
929 N. Water St.
Milwaukee, WI 53202

DINNER THEATRES

Arizona
Windmall Dinner Theatre
10345 N. Scottsdale Rd.
Scottsdale, AZ 85253

California
Sebastian's Grand Dinner Theatre
Grand Hotel
One Hotel Way
Anaheim, CA 92802

Lyric Dinner Theatre
7578 El Cajon Blvd.
La Mesa, CA 92041

Sebastian's West Dinner Theatre
140 Avenida Pico
San Clemente, CA 92672

Harlequin Dinner Playhouse
3503 S. Harbor Blvd.
Santa Ana, CA 92704

Fiesta Dinner Theatre
9665 Campo Rd.
Spring Valley, CA 92077

Colorado
Country Dinner Playhouse
6875 S. Clinton
Englewood, CO 80110

Connecticut
Darien Dinner Theatre
65 Tokeneke Rd.
Darien, CT 06820

Dinner Theatres (continued)

Coachlight Dinner Theatre
266 Main St.
Warehouse Point, CT 06088

Florida
Royal Palm Dinner Theatre
303 Gulf View Dr.
Royal Palm Plaza
Boca Raton, FL 33432

Alhambra Dinner Theatre
12000 Beach Blvd.
Jacksonville, FL 32216

Burt Reynolds Dinner Theatre
1001 Indiantown Rd.
Jupiter, FL 33458

Oakland West Dinner Theatre
4850 W. Oakland Park Blvd.
Lauderdale Lakes, FL 33313

Naples Dinner Theatre
1025 Piper Blvd.
Naples, FL 33940

Showboat Dinner Theatre
3405 Ulmerton Rd.
P.O. Box 519
Pinellas Park, FL 33565

Country Dinner Playhouse
7951 Gateway Mall
9th St. North
St. Petersburg, FL 33702

Golden Apple Dinner Theatre
25 N. Pineapple Ave.
Sarasota, FL 33577

Illinois
Pheasant Run Cabaret Theatre
Box 64
St. Charles, IL 60174

Candlelight Dinner Playhouse
5620 S. Harlem Ave.
Summit, IL 60501

Indiana
Derby Dinner Theatre
525 Marriot Dr.
Clarksville, IN 47130

Beef 'n' Boards Dinner Theatre
9301 W. Michigan
P.O. Box 68329
Indianapolis, IN 46268

Louisiana
Beverly Dinner Playhouse
217 LaBarre Rd.
Jefferson, LA 70121

Maryland
New Bolton Hill Dinner Theatre
1111 Park Ave.
Baltimore, MD 21201

Limestone Valley Dinner Theatre
P.O. Box 123
Cockeysville, MD 21030

Minnesota
Chanhassen Dinner Theatre
Chanhassen, MN 55317

Missouri
Waldo Astoria Dinner Theatre
7428 Washington
Kansas City, MO 64114

Nebraska
Firehouse Dinner Theatre
514 S. 11th St.
Omaha, NE 68102

New Mexico
Barn Dinner Theatre
P.O. Box 257
Cedar Crest, NM 87008

New York
An Evening Dinner Theatre
11 Clearbrook Rd.
Elmsford, NY 10523

Dinner Theatres (continued)

Lake George Dinner Theatre
P.O. Box 266
Lake George, NY 12845

North Carolina
Village Dinner Theatre
Route 1, Box 430
Morrisville, NC 27560

Ohio
Beef 'n' Boards Dinner Theatre
9660 Dry Fork Rd.
P.O. Box 226
Harrison, OH 45030

Canal Fulton Dinner Theatre
P.O. Box 427
Ravenna, OH 44266

Carousel Dinner Theatre
P.O. Box 427
Ravenna, OH 44266

Country Dinner Theatre
7370 Tussing Rd.
Reynoldsburg, OH 44266

Westgate Dinner Theatre
Westgate Village
3301 W. Central Ave.
Toledo, OH 43606

South Carolina
Act II Dinner Theatre
Fawn Vista North
Deerfield Plantation
Myrtle Beach, SC 29577

Texas
Country Squire Dinner Theatre
P.O. Box 30520
Amarillo, TX 79120

Country Dinner Playhouse
11829 Abrams Rd.
Dallas, TX 75231

Granny's Dinner Playhouse
12205 Coit Rd.
Dallas, TX 75251

Windmill Dinner Theatre
5531 Yale Blvd.
Dallas, TX 75206

Fiesta Dinner Playhouse
1270 N. Loop, #1604E
San Antonio, TX 78232

Virginia
Hayloft Dinner Theatre
10501 Balls Ford Rd.
Manassas, VA 22110

Washington
Cirque Dinner Theatre
131 Taylor Ave., North
Seattle, WA 98109

Davenport Hotel
(Arena Room)
W. 807 Sprague Ave.
Spokane, WA 99204

STOCK THEATRES

Colorado
Elitch Gardens Theatre
4620 W. 38th St.
Denver, CO 80212
(COST)

Connecticut
Summer Stage
Trinity College
Hartford, CT 06106
(CORST)

Stock Theatres (continued)

Sharon Playhouse
Route 396
Sharon, CT 06069
(CORST)

Westport Country Playhouse
25 Powers Court
P.O. Box 629
Westport, CT 06880
(COST)

Illinois

Drury Lane Theatre South
2500 W. 94th Pl.
Evergreen Park, IL 60642
(COST)

Marriott's Lincolnshire Resort Theatre
101 Half Day Rd.
Lincolnshire, IL 60015
(COST)

Shady Lane Playhouse
Route #20 West
Marengo, IL 60152
(CORST)

Little Theatre On The Square
P.O. Box 159
Sullivan, IL 61951
(COST)

Woodstock Performing Company
P.O. Box 190
Woodstock, IL 60098
(CORST)

Maine

Ogunquit Playhouse
Ogunquit, ME 03907
(COST)

Lakewood Theatre
P.O. Box 99
Skownegan, ME 04976
(CORST)

Maryland

Olney Theatre
Route 108
Olney, MD 20832
(COST)

Massachusetts

The Charles Playhouse
76 Warrenton St.
Boston, MA 02116
(COST)

North Shore Music Theatre
P.O. Box 62
Beverly, MA 01915
(CORST)

Cape Playhouse
Dennis, MA 02638
(COST)

Falmouth Playhouse
Falmouth, MA 02541
(COST)

Berkshire Theatre Festival
Berkshire Playhouse
E. Main St.
Stockbridge, MA 01262
(CORST)

Williamstown Theatre Festival
Adams Memorial Theatre
Main St.
P.O. Box 517
Williamstown, MA 01267
(CORST)

Michigan

Barn Theatre
Route #1, M-96
Augusta, MI 49012
(CORST)

Minnesota

Old Log Theatre
Box 250
Excelsior, MN 55331
(CORST)

Stock Theatres (continued)

New Hampshire

Hampton Playhouse
Winnacunnett Rd.
Hampton, NH 03842
(CORST)

Gilford Playhouse
c/o Star Theatre Productions
P.O. Box 1100
Laconia, NH 03246
(COST)

American Stage Festival
P.O. Box 225
Milford, NH 03055
(CORST)

Peterborough Playhouse
Off Middle Hancock Rd.
P.O. Box 1
Peterborough, NH 03458
(CORST)

The Barnstormers
Tamworth, NH 03886
(CORST)

New York

Corning Summer Theatre
P.O. Box 51
Corning, NY 14830
(COST)

John Drew Theatre
158 Main St.
East Hampton, NY 11937
(COST)

Olmstead Theatre
Adelphi University
Garden City, NY 11530
(CORST)

Woodstock Playhouse
P.O. Box 396
Woodstock, NY 12498
(CORST)

Pennsylvania

Allenberry Playhouse
Boiling Springs, PA 17007
(CORST)

Totem Pole Playhouse
Caledonia State Park
Fayetteville, PA 17222
(CORST)

Mountain Playhouse
Jennerstown, PA 15547
(CORST)

Pocono Playhouse
Mountainhome, PA 19432
(COST)

Vermont

St. Michael's Playhouse
56 College Pkwy.
Winooski, VT 05404
(CORST)

Wisconsin

Peninsula Players
Hwy. 42
Fishcreek, WI 54212
(CORST)

Appendix E

GLOSSARY

Academy Players Directory: Publication in Hollywood which contains actors' photos and lists agent/or agents who represent them. The directory is published three times a year. An actor must be a member of one of the acting unions or be represented by a franchised agent in order to be listed in the directory.

Actors' Equity Association (AEA): Also known as "Equity." Equity is the union which has jurisdiction over stage performers and stage managers.

actors' syndrome: "Illness" an actor might acquire after many "No"s on auditions and interviews. The disease stems from the "nobody wants me" attitude.

age range: Ages that an actor can possibly play. This range can, but doesn't necessarily have to, include the actor's real age.

agent: Person who represents the actor. The agent is responsible for getting the actor on auditions and interviews, and for negotiating the actor's contracts with employers.

American Dinner Theatre Institute (ADTI): Located in Sarasota, Florida. ADTI is a clearinghouse for Equity dinner theatres all over the country. It supplies news and information of interest to the dinner theatres and negotiates Equity dinner theatre contracts on their behalf.

121

American Federation of Television and Radio Artists (AFTRA): Union which includes jurisdiction over performers in live and taped TV shows (newscasters and announcers included), taped commercials, radio shows, and phonograph records.

audition: Meeting with casting director (and others) at which an actor reads for a part; term generally associated with stage. Auditions for TV, film, and commercial roles are generally referred to as "interviews."

Backstage: Show Biz magazine published weekly in New York. Though it's primarily for the New York area, it also contains a regional section for other parts of the U.S. It lists casting calls and other general information of interest to the actor.

billing: Credit line attached to the actor's name for a particular role ("Star," "Guest Star," "Co-Star," "Featuring," "Introducing," etc.).

Breakdown Services: A publication with New York and Hollywood editions, that lists roles being cast for TV and film. It is distributed daily (except weekends) to franchised union agents and managers.

call-back: A return to an audition or interview to be seen again.

casting director: Person who casts minor roles and generally screens actors who will potentially meet the director and/or producer for the larger roles.

cattle calls: Interviews and auditions in which hundreds of actors are seen in a very short period of time. The name comes from the practice of lining up cows and picking out the beefiest ones for selling.

Chicago Off-Loop Theatre (COLT): Equity theatres and contracts in the Chicago area. COLT contracts generally have lower wage minimums due to their smaller audiences.

client: In theatrical work, generally refers to the actor in his relationship with the agent. The relationship is often referred to as the "agent/client" relationship. In commercial work, "client" generally refers to the advertiser sponsoring the commercial.

cold reading: Type of reading for which the actor is given very little, if any, rehearsal time before performing the material. Most TV, film, and commercial interviews include a cold reading.

Commercial Breakthrough/In-Touch: A computerized service, in Los Angeles, which sends messages each day to teleprinters in commercial agents' offices, providing information about casting calls.

composite: Group of photos arranged on an 8½" x 11" sheet of lithograph paper that shows the actor or model in different situations. In New York and Hollywood, composites generally are used only for commercials and not for theatrical (TV, stage, and film) pictures. (Exception: Sometimes children's agents will use them for theatrical as well as commercial pictures.)

Council of Resident Stock Theatres (CORST): Negotiating body for Equity resident dramatic stock theatres all over the country. To be considered a stock company the theatre must be producing two or more plays simultaneously. CORST theatres maintain a nucleus of performers from one play to the next.

Council of Stock Theatres (COST): Negotiating body for Equity non-resident dramatic stock companies all over the country. To be considered a stock company the theatre must be producing two or more plays simultaneously. The main difference between CORST and COST is that COST is a non-resident company and CORST is a resident company (i.e., maintains a nucleus of players from one play to the next).

cover letter: Letter sent along with an actor's picture and resume to agents and casting directors.

Drama-Logue: Show Biz magazine published weekly in Hollywood. Though it's primarily for the Hollywood area, it also contains a regional section for other parts of the U.S. It lists casting calls and other general information of interest to the actor.

Equity. See *Actors' Equity Association.*

Equity Waiver: Term used for stage productions in Hollywood for which the theatre has "99 seats or less," and the actors don't get paid. These plays are showcase plays for the actor and do come under Equity jurisdiction. Both Equity and non-Equity members may perform in such plays.

extra: In TV and film work, a player who doesn't speak any lines; generally referred to as "background" or "atmosphere." In commercial work, however, an actor might be considered a principal player (not an extra) whether he speaks a line or not. If the actor is on-camera and is identified with the product, demonstrates the product, or reacts to the message in the commercial, he might be considered a principal without mouthing a word. The determination can become touchy, and many times SAG has had to view the commercial to decide who is a principal and who is an extra. If someone is a true extra in an Equity stage production (speaks no lines) and isn't an understudy, then he's paid one-half of the regular actor's salary under that contract, though stage actors who don't speak any lines or speak only a few lines are generally understudies for the larger roles and under those circumstances would be paid their regular salary.

franchised: Refers to agents who have signed contracts with the various acting unions. If an agent isn't franchised, that agent isn't "legit"; he can't negotiate actors' contracts with union productions.

freelancing: Refers to an actor representing himself instead of having agency representation.

general interview: Interview in which an actor might just talk to the casting director, director, producer, etc. The interviewer might not even be casting any particular project at that moment. It's a "get-acquainted" type of meeting that could lead to interviews for specific projects in the future.

head shot: an 8″ x 10″ photo that is used mostly for stage, TV, and film roles. The head shot is rarely, if ever, used for commercials, though it is often included on the commercial composite. The picture is usually taken from the middle of the bustline or shoulders up.

holding fee: In commercials, fee that is given to the actor even though his commercial isn't presently airing. The fee is in compensation for the fact that the actor can't be in any other commercials for any product that competes with the original product during a specified period of time.

Hollywood Area Theatre/Bay Area Theatre (HAT/BAT): Type

of Equity theater contract used for the Hollywood and San Francisco areas. These contracts generally have lower wage minimums for the actors due to their smaller audiences.

Hollywood Reporter: Show Biz magazine published daily (excluding weekends) in Hollywood. It is distributed in many areas, but its primary concern is with Hollywood. Though it's basically a business magazine, it often includes casting news of interest to the actor.

interview: In the screen world, refers to auditions for TV, film, and commercial roles. In stage acting, refers to a meeting between the actor and the people responsible for casting the production. Generally referred to as the "Equity Principal Interview" where no actual readings take place. This is a get-acquainted session where the actor brings his photograph and resume and chats with the personnel holding the interview.

League of Resident Theatres (LORT): Negotiating body for Equity resident theatres all over the country. To be considered a resident theatre the theatre must be producing a series of plays. The difference between LORT theatres and other resident theatres is that LORT theatres are non-profit organizations.

manager: Person who represents the actor but who isn't franchised by the unions and is *not* considered an agent. The manager operates more in a managing capacity than in a negotiating capacity. His fee is usually anywhere from ten to twenty-five percent of the actor's salary, but there are no limits.

matching: Refers to "physically" being right for a part. If the producer is casting, for example, roles for a family, then the family would have to "match" each other. This term is used more for TV, film, and commercials than for stage.

monologue: Dramatic sketch given by one actor alone. Generally it is used for stage auditions rather than for screen interviews.

network approval: Refers to a television network approving a certain actor for a project being handled by its studio. Network approval is usually only needed for major roles, if at all.

non-Equity: Type of play production which isn't under the jurisdiction of Actors' Equity Association. Equity members may not participate in this type of production.

non-SAG: Type of film or filmed TV production that isn't under the jurisdiction of the Screen Actors Guild. Members of SAG may not participate in this type of production.

Off-Broadway (in reference to Equity contracts): Type of Equity contract used for Off-Broadway theatres in New York. These contracts usually have lower wage minimums because of the smaller houses in the Off-Broadway market.

padding: Adding irrelevant, unimportant, or inaccurate information to a resume to make it look more impressive. A no-no for actors.

Players Guide: Publication in New York which contains actors' photos and lists agent/or agents who represent them. The guide is published once a year, and is used mainly by producers and casting directors.

principal player: Under SAG jurisdiction, anyone who speaks a line of dialogue on or off camera. Under AFTRA jurisdiction, anyone who speaks a line if he is in a situation comedy, and anyone who speaks over five lines if he's in a variety show. In commercials, under both unions, anyone who speaks a line of dialogue, or anyone whose face appears while demonstrating or illustrating the product, or anyone whose face is shown reacting to the message in the commercial.

principal role: Role that falls into the category described in the above definition of "principal player."

producer: In television, individual(s) totally responsible to the network for the finished product of the show. In movies and stage, the producer is totally responsible to the backers for the finished product. The producer is in charge of hiring the casting director, director, actors, technical crew heads, etc. He handles the financial responsibilities as well.

product conflict: In commercials, means that the actor has two commercials airing, or for which he's being "held," and the products compete with each other in the marketplace.

Production Contract: Standard contract used for any single Equity production. The Production Contract has the highest-paying minimum contract for the actor.

residual: A payment to the actor for each re-airing of a commercial or TV show after the initial airing.

rounds: Refers to stage actors dropping off their pictures and resumes at casting directors', directors', or producers' offices. Term generally used in New York more so than in other cities.

Screen Actors Guild (SAG): Union for actors which has jurisdiction over films, filmed TV shows, and filmed commercials.

Screen Extras Guild (SEG): Union for "background" or "atmosphere" actors, people who do not speak any lines in feature films, filmed TV shows, and filmed commercials, in cities in which SEG has offices. (Does not apply to stage.)

Show Business: Show Biz magazine published weekly in New York. Though the magazine has subscribers all over the U.S., it is primarily for the New York area. It lists casting information and other news of interest to the actor.

Showcase Code: Agreement used for showcase plays in New York for Off-Off Broadway theatres—theatres which have "99 seats or less." Any actor, Equity or non-Equity, may audition for these plays.

showcase plays: Plays which are produced for the benefit of the actors, writers, or directors (but generally for the benefit of the actors). There is no pay for such plays. In Hollywood, these plays are called "Equity Waiver" plays, and in New York they're called "Off-Off Broadway" plays under the "Showcase Code." Agents and casting directors attend such plays.

sign-in sheet: In commercials, refers to the sheet of paper each actor signs as he enters the interview. The actor signs his name, his agent's name and phone number, his own social security number, the time he arrives for the interview, and the time he leaves the interview.

slating: The stating of the actor's name and agent who represents him, on camera, during an interview for TV, film, or commercials.

submit (submission): Term referring to the sending out of a picture or resume by an agent or individual to the casting director, director, or producer, in the hopes of getting the actor an audition or interview.

Taft-Hartley: Law stating that a person can work a certain amount of time on a union job without having to join that union. As it typically applies to the acting unions, an actor can work up to thirty calendar days on his first job without joining the appropriate union. However, on his second job, or any job that he obtains after thirty calendar days, or any job that lasts over thiry calendar days, he must join if he wants to work on a show under that particular union.

test-market: In reference to commercials, the testing of a commercial in front of an audience to see what types of response the commercial receives from that audience.

Theatre Communications Group (TCG): Non-profit organization in New York, set up by the Ford Foundation as a clearinghouse for many resident theatres. TCG helps these theatres in casting, by holding invitational auditions for the specific plays. An invitation to one of these specific auditions depends on the actor's performance at TCG general auditions, which are usually held twice a year.

Theatre for Young Audiences (TYA): Type of Equity contract used for children's plays. These plays are usually performed in the daylight hours, and aren't over an hour-and-a-half in length.

type: Refers to physical characteristics of the actor. A casting director might want, for example, an "all-American" type.

under five: Under AFTRA contract, an actor who has a speaking role of five lines or fewer.

unsolicited: Usually refers to material (picture and resume) sent to a casting director, director, producer, etc., by an actor rather than by an agent.

Variety: Show Biz magazine published weekly and daily (two different versions). The weekly is an international issue published in New York, while the daily is published in Hollywood and is primarily for the Hollywood area. Though they are both basically business magazines, they do include casting news.

voice-over: Type of work in which the actor isn't seen, but his voice is heard.

wrap: Refers to the ending of the shooting day. Used more in TV, film, and commercial shooting than in stage work.

ABBREVIATIONS:

ADTI: American Dinner Theatre Institute
AEA: Actors' Equity Association (also known as Equity)
AFTRA: American Federation of Television and Radio Artists
AGMA: American Guild of Musical Artists
AGVA: American Guild of Variety Artists
COLT: Chicago Off-Loop Theatre
CORST: Council of Resident Stock Theatres
COST: Council of Stock Theatres
HAT/BAT: Hollywood Area Theatre/Bay Area Theatre
LORT: League of Resident Theatres
SAG: Screen Actors Guild
SEG: Screen Extras Guild
TCG: Theatre Communications Group
TYA: Theatre for Young Audiences

ABOUT THE AUTHOR

Tom Logan was born in Shreveport, Louisiana. His acting debut was at age 8, in Shreveport, where he performed in plays until he graduated from high school and left town to begin his college education. He performed in over fifty community theatre and college stage productions at such places as Centenary College, the University of Arkansas, the University of California at Santa Barbara, and California State University in Northridge. He graduated cum laude from the latter, with a B.A. degree in Theatre Arts.

In between his various college enrollments, Tom performed in many professional stage productions, among them "Applause" and "Mame" in the state of New York, "You're a Good Man, Charlie Brown" playing Schroeder, and "Androcles and the Lion" playing Androcles; the latter two he toured. In other words, much acting, little eating.

Deciding he wanted to eat more often, he moved to California to try for work in the screen medium while finishing work on his college degree. He has co-starred in several films, including "Massacre at Central High" (*New York Times* 20 Best Film List, 1980), starred in "Breakthrough," and is featured in several films, including "The Beach Girls." He has had co-starring roles on episodes of many prime-time TV series, including "CHiPs" (NBC), "James at 16" (NBC), "The Hardy Boys" (ABC), and "Project UFO" (NBC). He has had feature roles on many shows, including "What's Happening" (ABC), "CPO Sharkey" (NBC), "The National Disaster Survival Test" (NBC), "Dusty's Treehouse" (CBS), and the NBC two-part movie "The Best Place to Be." And he has appeared on the TV soap operas "General Hospital," "Days of Our Lives," and "The Young and Restless."

To assist in his goal of acting and eating at the same time, Logan has performed in many national commercials, including McDonald's, Ford, Honda, Coppertone, and Kodak. From that experience, Tom has learned numerous techniques for gaining success in the commercial acting field. He passes along many of these "secrets" in his second book, *ACTING IN THE MILLION DOLLAR MINUTE: The Art & Business of Performing in TV Commercials,* to be published by Communications Press in early 1984.

Though Logan manages to eat from his acting, he also lectures on the business of acting to students at various studios in Los Angeles.